The
Connell Guide
to

———————

The
American Novel
1880 - 1940

———————

by Stephen Fender

Contents

Introduction

In the 1950s half a dozen clever American scholars attempted to define the nature and character of American literature. Each of them saw something distinctive about it and their studies make fascinating, and instructive, reading.

Henry Nash Smith, in *Virgin Land: The American West as Symbol and Myth* (1950), examined the way the western frontier shaped American society and captivated its imagination with the apparent promise of vast, empty tracts of country. It's hard to exaggerate the importance of this idea, an idea present in one way or another in all the great American novels we look at in this book. From their first settlement on the continent Americans were acutely aware of being on a frontier; they felt a mixture of exhilaration about starting again in a new world and anxiety about leaving the old one behind. The idea of escape towards the west, away from the centres of civilisation in Europe and the more settled parts of the American east, fired the imagination, as well it might.

R.W.B. Lewis, in *The American Adam* (1955), developed this theme, stressing above all the extent to which American culture was shaped primarily by its sense of being "new" – and by a conscious desire to distance itself from the fusty traditions, habits and ways of thinking of the Old World. Perry Miller, in *Errand into the Wilderness* (1956), echoes this but pays particular attention to the religious dimension: Americans had come to New England, says Miller, as part of a mission to found a reformed society, free of the messy compromises and time-worn rituals which, in American eyes, beset the English church.

A year later, a fourth scholar, Richard Chase, weighed in with his highly influential *The American Novel and its Tradition* (1957). Boldly, Chase characterised classical American fiction as a kind of "romance". In traditional literary terms, romances are tales of the exploits of heroic figures – often in exotic settings. (The stories of King Arthur and his knights are medieval romances.) American romances, said Chase, essentially evoke the "radical forms of alienation... and disorder" inherent in living in a New World. Many great American novels, he thought, are not realistic in the sense that great English novels like, say, *Middlemarch* are realistic: they are interested less in the development of character in a tightly knit domestic world than in the momentous struggles of brave or daring individuals in a hostile environment, of man alone taking on the universe – the most famous example being that quintessential American story, Herman Melville's *Moby Dick* (1851).

Chase's thesis is ingenious but overstated. Most culpably, it ignores not only the vastly underestimated Edith Wharton but one of the greatest of all novelists, American or otherwise, Henry James. Both James and Wharton were profoundly interested in the development of character and in the minute observation of the way people behave. Both, of course, were shaped as much by their exposure to European culture as by their American origins, which is partly what sets them apart from their contemporaries. Indeed James once complained to Edith Wharton that it was impossible to set a wholly realistic novel – or "novel of manners" – in America. American society, he implied, was too new, too superficial. Producing a novel about it remained "a deadly difficulty". James's solution, and up to a point Wharton's, was to write fictions in which Americans found themselves encountering, blundering into, perhaps even getting the better of, the elaborate social codes that their European forebears had left behind them.

But while his definition is too rigid, Chase undoubtedly identifies an important strand in American fiction. Many American novels do indeed pit individuals against a hostile universe and, invariably, the universe wins. Romances, at least romances as defined by Chase, tend to go wrong. As another great US critic, Lionel Trilling, put it in *The Liberal Imagination* (1950):

> In the American metaphysic, reality is always material reality, hard, resistant, unformed, impenetrable and unpleasant. And that mind is alone felt to be trustworthy which most resembles this reality by most nearly reproducing the sensations it affords.

In other words, American naturalist authors felt that they were never more faithful to the truth than when their characters came to a bad end. So Stephen Crane's *Maggie: A Girl of the Streets* (1893) follows a girl from childhood to her young adult years. Seduced by a bartender, she is turned out by her mother, tries to make a living as a prostitute, and finally throws herself into the East River. Frank Norris's *McTeague* (1899) is about a California gold miner turned dentist in San Francisco, who kills his wife, provoking the wrath of a jealous rival who tracks him to Death Valley, where he slips a pair of handcuffs on him, only to be killed by McTeague. So McTeague dies of thirst and exposure, handcuffed to the man he has killed.

THE STORY OF CAPTAIN SMITH AND POCHAHONTAS

One of the first explorers of the New World was Captain John Smith (1580 – 1631), the leader of the English Virginia Colony at Jamestown, Virginia. In *The General History of Virginia* (1624), Smith describes how he heroically explores the wilderness, confronts and defeats the natives, and wins the heart of Pocahontas, the daughter of the native chief. His *General History* is a sort of renaissance pageant in which a European prince conquers and colonises the wild men of the New World. Pocahontas's love for her English hero is a figurative marriage of American nature and European culture, with the best of Europe transforming, and being renewed by, the best of America.

All of the remarkable studies we have considered above set out to frame American literature, for the first time, as a subject for debate and study. And all of them are highly flattering to their subject. There is, however, one important and highly controversial exception. The exception is Leslie Fiedler's *Love and Death in the American Novel* (1960). This was just as original as the studies which preceded it, but it was so far from flattering that it drew howls of outrage from contemporary critics, including Chase.

Though about as far apart as two critics can be, Fiedler and Chase agree on one fundamental issue. Both believe American novelists of the period we are studying were ill at ease with the kind of realism

But to succeed Smith has largely cut himself off from the Old World. And while he is out exploring the wilderness (as he tells it), confronting the Indians and at length winning them over, back at the makeshift camp established by the English on first landing in Virginia, his cowardly social betters are lounging about, squabbling among themselves, and – worst of all – threatening more than once to abandon the whole enterprise and high-tail it for home.

So in one of America's founding narratives the hero measures the success of his venture by the distance he travels from his European base. The frontier proclaims a value that is moral as well as geographical. And frontier heroes maintained their popularity in American fiction and folklore well into the 20th century. Think of any western hero, from the explorer and frontiersman Daniel Boone to the archetypal lonesome cowboy-gunfighter Shane, unable to settle down with the Starrett family even though they love him and he them. ▪

central to the 19th century English novel. The difference, however, was that to Fiedler this meant they simply couldn't write fiction for grown-ups. In classic American novels, he said, heterosexual love between adults was typically displaced by homoerotic relationships between white men or white boys and black men. As examples he gave Natty Bumppo and Chingachgook in Fenimore Cooper's *Leatherstocking Tales* (1823 – 41), Ishmael and Queequeg in *Moby Dick* and Huck and Jim in *Adventures of Huckleberry Finn*.

By this he didn't mean that the male characters were having sex together; in fact, the absence of sex was the salient point. What Fiedler was saying, as he put it in *Love and Death in the American Novel*, was that these and other novelists were substituting a childlike view of human relationships for adult, heterosexual love.

The typical male protagonist of our fiction has been a man on the run, harried into the forest and out to sea, down the river or into combat – anywhere to avoid "civilization," which is to say, the confront- ation of a man and woman which leads in the fall to sex, marriage, and responsibility.

Fiedler's attack was a salutary counterweight to the more indulgent view of his contemporaries. What made it especially significant, and brave, was that it appeared at a time when America had emerged, after World War Two, as the most powerful and self-confident country in the world. In this context, his assault seemed almost sacreligious. Was it fair? Up to a point, yes, though as we shall see in the chapters which follow, it does less than justice to some of the greatest American novels of the late 19th and early 20th centuries.

The Portrait of a Lady

Isabel Archer, a spirited and beautiful young American woman, is invited by her aunt Lydia Touchett to visit her estranged husband, Isabel's uncle Daniel, a wealthy banker, at Gardencourt, their country house near London. There she meets their son, her cousin Ralph, with whom she forms a deep friendship, and the intelligent and engaging Lord Warburton, one of whose large estates lies nearby. Warburton falls instantly in love with Isabel, but she turns his proposal down because she thinks accepting it would prevent her fulfilling her destiny. She also refuses her ardent American suitor, Caspar Goodwood, who has followed her to England.

While in London with her friend, the American journalist Henrietta Stackpole, Isabel learns that Daniel Touchett is seriously ill. She hurries back to Gardencourt to find another house guest there, a friend of her aunt's, the mysterious Madame Merle. Ralph prevails upon his father to bequeath a large part of his wealth to Isabel, because, as he says, "I should like to put a little wind in her sails".

Now the heiress to a large fortune, Isabel takes off for a tour of Europe. In Florence Madame Merle introduces her to Gilbert Osmond, a man of no profession but of exquisite taste, whom at length, and against the advice of all her friends and family, she determines to marry.

The couple set themselves up in Rome, in the menacing Palazzo Roccanera. They have a son, who lives only six months, but even before then the marriage has begun to go wrong, with Osmond coming increasingly to value Isabel as a social ornament only, while resenting and fearing her independence of mind.

Osmond has a daughter, Pansy, whom he keeps in a convent. When she is courted by a young American art collector called Rosier, Isabel tries to help the mutually attracted couple, but Osmond objects strenuously on the grounds that Rosier isn't sufficiently rich or socially elevated. At this point

THE RADICAL CHANGES IN AMERICAN SOCIETY

The years from 1880 to 1940 brought more rapid and radical changes than any other six decades in American history, before or since. In 1880 most people (around 60 per cent of the population) were living on farms – and the rest in cities; by 1940 this proportion was almost exactly reversed. More than 30 million immigrants had arrived in the country, and the overall population had more than doubled.

In 1880 public transport was by riverboat or on the nation's early railroads, while locally people got around on

Lord Warburton reappears on the scene. Both Osmond and Madame Merle want him for Pansy, and knowing of his love for Isabel, ask her to help. She suspects that Warburton is more interested in her than Pansy, to which he admits. Osmond and Merle are furious.

Ralph is seriously ill at Gardencourt. Osmond forbids Isabel from going to him, but she defies him, promising Pansy that she will not abandon her. Ralph dies. Goodwood appears again, kissing her passionately and begging Isabel to come away with him, but Isabel decides to return to Rome.

Isabel Archer is one of Henry James's American girls. Said to be based on an idealised version of Minny Temple, his beloved cousin who died young, James's American girls are beautiful, well brought up, clever, independent, and usually rich.

They have the wit and confidence to challenge accepted standards, even (perhaps especially) if these

horseback or in buckboards and carriages over dirt roads. By 1940 mass movement was in fast trains and airliners, and more than 80 per cent of American households owned a car. Over the same time electric lighting, the radio, telephones and the moving pictures were introduced.

So by 1940 America had urbanised, modernised, centralised, diversified. In 1880 it had recently been torn apart by a terrible civil war, then uneasily reunited; by 1940, apart from enduring a traumatic depression, it had been through its first European war, and was about to be thrust into another, much greater, global struggle which would end with it becoming, indisputably, the most powerful country in the world. ■

are traditional and European. But not always the knowledge: "She thinks she knows a great deal of [the world]," Mrs Touchett says of Isabel, "but like most American girls she's ridiculously mistaken." Yet as the narrator puts it, "Isabel Archer was a young person of many theories", a "remarkably active" imagination and a tendency "to care for knowledge that was tinged with the unfamiliar". Among those theories was that "Isabel Archer was very fortunate in being independent, and that she ought to make some very enlightened use of that state".

Towards the end of Chapter Seven, Mrs Touchett criticises Isabel for having sat up one night talking to Ralph and Lord Warburton. "Young girls here – in decent houses – don't sit alone with the gentlemen late at night," she tells her. Mystified, Isabel asks Mrs. Touchett to keep her informed of the things she shouldn't do. "So as to do them?" asks her aunt. "So as to choose," Isabel replies.

And how does Isabel exercise her choice? By marrying Osmond. This has baffled readers, as it has critics. For the English critic, Tony Tanner, the reason is partly that Osmond is the least sexy of her suitors. Isabel, he says, is driven by fear: she is "frightened of sexual passion, of her unexpected wealth, of her 'freedom'". Of her various offers, "Caspar Goodwood suggests oppression, coercion and constraint on the plain physical level. Lord Warburton, with his complex social relations and obligations, suggests immobilisation on the social level."

A charcoal drawing of Henry James by John Singer Sargent (1912)

But why Osmond, of all people? Isabel thinks that "life can be lived as pure spirit in contempt of things", which is what attracts her to Osmond, Tanner says, but what she doesn't realise is that Osmond "has spiritualised the material".

The American critic Millicent Bell is less critical of Isabel. Bell thinks her main motive for marrying Osmond is the same as Ralph's in arranging her inheritance.

Her benevolence, like Ralph's, results from her

own incapacity to use money directly. This incapacity is literal; as a woman she has no way to make money 'work,' since women of her type and time are only consumers.

What Isabel admires in Osmond is above all his good taste. Her mistake, as Dorothea Krook, astutely points out, is in thinking that his exquisite discrimination in *things* extends to his moral choices. "Isabel has to suffer, and through her suffering learn that the aesthetic is not coextensive with the moral, and that the touchstone of taste is not the touchstone by which a good life can be lived."

It is characteristic of this novel – in which thought, opinion and feelings are at least as important as physical action – that its climax should take place as Isabel sits alone and undisturbed by a dying fire. The devastating Chapter 42, in which she reviews the full horror of her marriage, is perhaps the most moving extended passage of free indirect speech in the language.* At this point she has already begun to gather that her husband's "more direct communication with Madame Merle than she suspected" is somehow mixed up in the Pansy business.

She then goes on to recapitulate the reasons for her original attraction to Osmond, the "charm" she had "been immensely under": his praise for her as "the most imaginative woman he had

* That is, when a narrator takes on the voice or manner of thinking of a character.

known"; his vulnerability; the immense lightening of her burdensome conscience at the thought that her money would empower Osmond's taste. And now her "cheek burn[s]" at the thought that she has married on such a "factitious theory". Reviewing her predicament, she reflects that far from valuing her imagination, Osmond thinks that "she has too many ideas and that she must get rid of them". As for his "taste", what is that but a snobbish "contempt for everyone but some three or four very exalted people whom he envied, and for everything in the world but half a dozen ideas of his own" and a slavish "esteem for tradition"?

Richard Chase greatly admires *The Portrait of a Lady*, despite its un-American interest and skill in the realistic development of character. This is because he recognises that James consciously assimilated elements of romance "into the novelistic substance" of the novel – in the language of the book and in the typical outlook of Isabel, who "tends to see things as a romancer does".

Certainly there are romance-like aspects of Isabel's predicament. She is virtually held prisoner in the Palazzo Roccanera ("black fortress") – like the Lady Lyonesse of Arthurian romance, captive in the Castle Perilous – and when she finally confronts Madame Merle (the name comes from the French word for "blackbird", colloquially associated in French with cunning and sharp practice), the evil she finds seems to her to be supernatural. "Who are you? *What* are you?" she demands of Merle, as she discovers her rival's full involvement with her husband.

So, of course, having defied Osmond and gone direct to Ralph's deathbed in England, she will refuse to return to the Palazzo Roccanera. Not a bit of it. Although Goodwood tracks her down even to the garden at Gardencourt, and plants a fiery kiss on her lips "like white lightening, a flash that spread, and spread again, and stayed", yet "when darkness returned" – that is, when the lightening had faded, as had the light in the garden – "she was free".

"I am not fully certain of James's intention here," writes Tony Tanner,

> but the effect is this. For a long time she has
> wondered if her true fate, the true realisation of
> her self, should not have been with Goodwood.
> Now for the first time she is subjected to the full
> force of his sexual claims, it is a shattering
> experience, but it is also a release.

Or maybe Goodwood came as a temporary reminder of one direction her life might have taken, a trajectory long rejected. This scene is here to tell us that Isabel is not immune to sexual attraction, let alone (now) afraid of it, but that she has underlying obligations, not just to her marriage vows, which in her time could not simply be cast aside, but also to Pansy, to whom she had promised to return. As Philip Horne, editor of the modern Penguin edition, has written, "although we are told that for her as she

Nicole Kidman as Isabel Archer in the 1996 film The Portrait of a Lady

escapes from Goodwood, 'There was a very straight path', we don't know quite why, or where it leads (and do all straight paths lead to Rome?)".

Millicent Bell thinks that Isabel's frame of mind at the book's end is best summed up, when she gets off the boat train at Charing Cross on her way to Gardencourt. "There was nothing to regret now – that was all over. Not only the time of her folly, but the time of her repentance seemed far away." What is more, Madame Merle has been banished to the America in which she had been born – a fate often assigned to Jamesian miscreants.

As for Isabel...

She saw herself, in the distant years, still in the attitude of a woman who had her life to live...

17

Deep in her soul – deeper than any appetite for renunciation – was the sense that life would be her business for a long time to come. And at moments there was something inspiring, almost exhilarating, in the conviction.

In "The Lesson of the Master", Henry James talks about his heroes and heroines as "artists", whose pre-eminent aim, always, is to do their best. The goal of each is the feeling "of having drawn from [his or her] intellectual instrument the finest music that nature had hidden in it". Isabel never thinks of her struggle in quite these terms but, as the critic David Galloway says, James saw her as "the figure of American innocence, of the nascent consciousness of a 'race'". And both the way James shapes her internal monologue, and the wider themes of the novel, are what we think of now as very modern. Galloway writes:

The Portrait of a Lady is distinctly a book about the failure to communicate, and the characters are repeatedly seen as isolated and rootless. The Touchett marriage has ended in separation; the first marriages of both Madame Merle and Gilbert Osmond have ended in death, and their own affair never results in marriage; Ralph, of course, never marries; and we suspect that Lord Warburton will make the sort of 'convenient' marriage which will never be able to offer him any deep personal fulfilment. Only Henrietta and the pliable, colourless Mr Banting seem to have anything like a happy personal relationship. The failure to communicate is imaged by Mrs Touchett's 'inscrutable' telegrams... Dramatically, the failure to communicate and hence the failure, for James, of life, is counterpointed by death – the slow death of Mr Touchett, the death of Isabel's infant son, and finally Ralph's own death.

Huckleberry Finn

Huck Finn, son of the town drunk, lives in a hogshead down at the tan-yard in a Missouri town on the Mississippi River. Mark Twain's *Tom Sawyer* (1876) ends with Tom and Huck discovering the dead body of the outlaw Injun Joe and unearthing his ill-gotten treasure. The money is divided between Huck and Tom and put out at 6% interest on their behalf. Huck is adopted by the widow Douglas, who will try to civilise him.

Huck feels confined living with the Widow and her sister Miss Watson, but is kidnapped by his father, who is after his money. Desperate to get away, Huck fakes his own death and lights out to Jackson's island in the middle of the Mississippi River. Here he meets up with Miss Watson's slave Jim, who has also escaped because he overheard her saying she was going to sell him down river to harsh servitude on a plantation.

The two become friends, deciding to set off together down river to Cairo, in the free state of Illinois, where the Ohio and Mississippi Rivers meet. At various points they are separated – as when a steamboat runs into their raft, splitting it in two, and Huck is offered shelter by the Grangerfords, a family who later get largely wiped out by the clan with whom they are engaged in a murderous feud – then gratefully reunited.

Their longest involvement is with a pair of conmen who style themselves as the sons of an English duke and the King of France. With the King and the Duke Huck and Jim are involved in a string of scams, at first just preposterous, then increasingly exploitative, until, to Huck's horror and disgust, the two sell Jim to a local farmer, who intends to claim the reward for returning him to Miss Watson.

It turns out the farmer and his family are related to Tom Sawyer, who comes down river and – after an elaborate charade of pretending to free Jim – reveals that he has been free all along, because Miss Watson has died and freed Jim in her will. Huck has had enough, and decides to "light out" for Indian Territory.

So Huck Finn is the very prototype of Leslie Fiedler's American narrative. He is "on the run... to avoid 'civilization'" and instead of getting to know the opposite sex with a view (eventually) to getting married and settling down, he bonds with a black man twice his age.

So much for the kind of fiction we're dealing

Mark Twain in 1907

with. But what about the quality? "All modern American literature comes from one book by Mark Twain called *Huckleberry Finn*," wrote Ernest Hemingway in *Green Hills of Africa* (1935). "There was nothing before. There has been nothing as good since." The book is good, first, in the invention of its central character, whose barely articulate moral sense prevents him from conforming not only to the manners and pieties of the "civilisation" around him, but also to its greed, prejudices and cruelties.

The book is also technically inventive. The story of *Tom Sawyer*, in keeping with the conventions of local-colour stories of good-bad boys up to that time, is told by an "educated" third-person narrator who mediates between the boys and their readers.

Adventures of Huckleberry Finn is told solely in the voice of the book's eponymous hero.

Having the story told by a narrator with limited consciousness was a risky departure, because it restricted the tonal range of the narrative. On the other hand, it gave plenty of scope for irony. From the start Mark Twain uses Huck's more restricted range of reference and his limited stylistic repertoire to convey a relatively naïve outlook, first on the town's prissy conventions, later on the wider world beyond it. The world looks strange through Huck's eyes, and since he is the only narrator, it is refreshed, made strange and new in the reader's eyes too. The familiar is de-familiarised by Huck's perception. After the widow takes him in:

> Well, then, the old thing commenced again. The widow rang a bell for supper, and you had to come to time. When you got to the table you couldn't go right to eating, but you had to wait for the widow to tuck down her head and grumble a little over the victuals, though there warn't really anything the matter with them. That is, nothing, only everything was cooked by itself. In a barrel of odds and ends it is different; things get mixed up, and juice kind of swaps around, and the things go better. (Chapter 1)

This is a funny, highly inventive sketch, an alien outlook on dinner bells, saying grace and food served as separate courses, but it is still just that: a sketch, a short item that might have filled a newspaper column. Later in the book Huck's naïve outlook, when he teams up with the escaped slave Jim, and they confront various levels of fraud and violence on their way downriver, will be put to darker, more satiric use.

But Huck doesn't take himself off to the woods just to escape from the town and its proprieties, or to test their values. On his second escape from the widow's constraints, he and Tom climb to the edge of the hill-top overlooking the town, "and could see three or four lights twinkling, where there was sick folks, may be; and the stars over us was sparkling ever so fine; and down by the village was the river, a whole mile broad, and awful still and grand."

This is a remarkable passage – not least technically. Mark Twain needs an expansive description of the superb landscape before them – together with a mention of the river, on which so much of the book's action will take place – yet, because of the first-person narrative, he has to work within Huck's limited repertoire. The trick is done by deploying sound Anglo-Saxonisms credibly within his narrator's range, words like "broad" and "awful still", which express the awe-inspiring immensity of this scene far more powerfully than could any amount of more educated prattling about sublime prospects. Huck, unlike the other boys, is stirred by this sudden opening of the natural world. And his imagination responds not only to landscapes but also to people; he alone has the humane sympathy to imagine that "there was sick folks, maybe" where the lights were still on in the houses below.

Not only Hemingway but Fiedler, Lionel Trilling and even the poet T. S. Eliot have considered *Adventures of Huckleberry Finn* to be a great book. Not so the modern novelist Jane Smiley, who thinks that the "greatness" of *Huckleberry Finn* is largely because critics have over-valued the work of white male authors (creating the so-called "white male canon"). "I don't hold any grudges against Huck himself," Smiley hastens to add. "He's just a boy trying to survive. The villain here is Mark Twain, who knew how to give Huck a voice but didn't know how to give him a novel."

The novel, she feels, suffers from a lack of verisimilitude. Why would Huck and Jim escape down river, running the risk of drifting past the confluence of the Ohio River (which they do) deep into plantation country where slaves are worked to death – the very fate Jim was trying to escape – when they could simply have crossed the Mississippi into Illinois in the first place?

This seems a rather pedestrian objection: the book is a novel, and Mark Twain is telling a picaresque tale of travel from Missouri to Kentucky, then into Arkansas, ever deeper into slaveholding country as the satire darkens, until the King sells Jim for $40 to get drunk on. The length of the journey – its interruptions, its reversals, its dangers – shapes the reader's experience of Huck's learning

An illustration for Huckleberry Finn *by E.W. Kemble*

and maturing.

A more valid criticism of the novel concerns its ending. In fact the ending is all wrong. Huck, we thought, had himself escaped from Tom's childish games of outlawry and banditry, when he left behind him the fantasy gang "ambuscading" the Sunday-school picnic of a school primary class, in order to set out as a real outlaw helping a slave really to escape. When Tom reappears on the scene full of elaborate, farcical ruses for "freeing" Jim, who is free already, we see he hasn't changed. He is the foil against which we measure Huck's development since he has been away on the raft.

But then Huck falls in with Tom's foolish schemes, as if the King and the Duke had taught him nothing about telling truth from falsehood. Finally, after no fewer than nine chapters of increasingly frustrating, sometimes tedious Tomfoolery, Huck has had enough. He lights out for the Territory. That, at least, is fitting.

"I believe that the ending of *Huckleberry Finn* makes so many readers uneasy because they rightly sense that it jeopardizes the significance of the entire novel," says Leo Marx. He's right. Even Hemingway thought that "If you read it you must stop where the Nigger Jim is stolen from the boys. That is the real end. The rest is just cheating." I agree. But despite the flawed ending Huck Finn is and remains the archetypal American hero, not just because of his need to flee settled society, but because through him Mark Twain shows that even an individual on the margins of society can be given not just a voice but a moral point of view.

Sister Carrie

A young woman brought up on an impoverished farm moves to Chicago to find work, then works her way up through the social and economic ranks of her lovers – first a travelling salesman called Charles Drouet, next George Hurstwood, the manager of a "way -up, swell" saloon with whom she runs away, first to Canada and then to New York. Finally, having become a successful actress, she begins to mix in the upper echelons of metropolitan society, while Hurstwood, out of work and gambling away his savings, winds up homeless on the streets of New York, finally committing suicide in a flophouse.

As this narrative introduction to Chapter Eight of *Sister Carrie* makes clear, Theodore Dreiser was right up to speed in the ideology of American naturalism:

> Among the forces which sweep and play throughout the universe, untutored man is but a wisp in the wind. Our civilization is still in a middle stage, scarcely beast... scarcely human... We see man far removed from the lairs of the jungles... too wise always to hearken to instincts and desires...

But *Sister Carrie* extends the logic of naturalism one step further than *McTeague*. Here the power that material circumstances have over human behaviour extends even to moral, spiritual and aesthetic choices. Carrie progresses up the ladder like a microcosm of Herbert Spencer's ameliorating society – not just the ladder of material wealth, but also the ladder of feeling, perception, intelligence, personal power. They all go together, as they most decidedly do not in the English 19th-century novel.

Indeed part of Dreiser's originality lies in his discovery that the material and spiritual are often indivisible. Look at this encounter between Carrie and her first seducer, Drouet. They have already met on the train to Chicago. Since then Carrie has been living with her sister and working virtuously, if miserably, in a shoe factory. Then she falls ill and loses her job. As she wanders the streets of the city cold, hungry and virtually penniless, she happens upon Drouet again, who immediately grasps the seriousness of her predicament, and forthwith takes her to a "large, comfortable" restaurant "with a substantial service". Soon he is ordering.

> 'Sirloin with mushrooms.' said Drouet. 'Stuffed tomatoes.'
> 'Yassuh,' assented the negro, nodding his head.
> 'Hashed brown potatoes.'
> 'Yessuh.'
> 'Asparagus.'
> 'Yassuh.'
> 'And a pot of coffee.'

When the food arrives, Drouet "helped Carrie to a rousing plateful and contributed the warmth of his spirit to her body" (VI).

This short passage tells us so much about Dreiser's imagination. First, he can understand the plight of a woman who contemporary public morality would condemn as "fallen" – or in the process of falling. She's hungry, lonely and cold, so of course she welcomes the support of a worldly companion in control of the mechanism to meet her basic needs. Second, he understood that the material and emotional were far from being opposed according to some moral programme, but that instead "the warmth of his spirit" grows out of a satisfyingly full meal.

Finally, more generally, Dreiser recognised that in this period of rapid social change, when so many people were migrating from country to city, what is truly "substantial" was changing. The farmstead, the traditional nuclear family, faith, and the ethical system based on these certainties – all cease to be substantial. Instead the adjective is associated with urban resorts of transient patronage, like a restaurant with "substantial" service, or the "gorgeous" saloon first described in Chapter Five, managed by Hurstwood, with his "solid, substantial air", produced, not by his character or behaviour, but by "his fine clothes, his clean linen, his jewels, and above all, his own sense of his importance".

But here is the real novelty: Carrie remains unpunished for her sexual transgressions, a feat that not even Tolstoy could manage in *Anna Karenina* (1878), in which the fallen protagonist finally throws herself under a train. Indeed the ending was so out of line that when Mrs Frank Doubleday heard about the book, she tried to prevent her husband from publishing it. He agreed with her, but could not break his contract with the author. In the event, the book came out unadvertised and sold only 456 copies of its original 1,008 print run.

"Carrie not only escaped punishment," says F. O. Matthiessen, "Dreiser did not even regard her as sinful; and this was the crux of his defiance of late nineteenth-century conventionality. Only he hardly thought of it then as a defiance. He was simply writing what he knew."

This is quite right. One of Dreiser's sisters ran away with a married saloon manager, while another took up with a rich man and bore his illegitimate child. But for Dreiser himself, as he wrote in *Dawn* (1931), his "Autobiography of Early Youth". Moral problems "such as the lives of my several sisters presented to me had no great weight". Visiting one sister's rooms, "[he] was filled with wonder at her clothes, furniture and the like, which seemed to contrast more than favorably with our own. [She] herself looked prosperous and cheerful."

More problematic was his prose style. It "seems as though he learned English from a newspaper", said F. R. Leavis. "He gives the feeling that he doesn't have any native language." Julian Markels agreed that "Dreiser's style is almost wholly unarticulated", but, unlike Leavis, thought this fulfilled a strategic purpose, in that "it simply affirms the inarticulateness of his characters".

The inarticulateness of the characters does seem to be part of the point. And this, too, makes a telling contrast with the classic English realistic novel, where moments of choice often constitute the climax of the action, since the story has been concerned with the protagonist's moral development. These pivotal moments are often signalled by the imagery of mirrors, in which the protagonists see themselves framed in their surroundings, providing a site for speculation (from the Latin *speculum*, mirror) and of course reflection.

Windows, too, work as an image for things as they are, providing a view on the world beyond the immediate preoccupations of the protagonist. Towards the end of *Middlemarch* the exhausted Dorothea falls asleep on the floor of her drawing room. The next morning, when she awakes and draws the curtains, she sees what might be called the vernacular world outside: a man with a bundle, a woman carrying her baby, a shepherd with his dog – generally "the manifold wakings of men to labour and endurance". It is now that Dorothea has her revelation:

> She was part of that involuntary, palpitating life, and could neither look out on it from her luxurious shelter as a mere spectator, nor hide her eyes in selfish complaining.

But look at the equivalent scenes in *Sister Carrie*. At the end of Chapter Twelve, just after Hurstwood has made his appeal to her interest and affection, Carrie looks into the mirror as she takes off her lace collar and undoes her "pretty alligator belt". "I'm getting terrible," she says. "I don't seem to do anything right... I don't know... what I can do." There is no insight here, no speculation, no reflection – only a hopeless vagueness as she gives in to the inevitable. Instead of the mirror, the piece of furniture to which she returns again and again in the novel is the rocking chair, which soothes her in its incessant reciprocal motion, going nowhere.

Instead of a window on the world, Hurstwood has the newspaper. When, with both Carrie and his savings gone, he reads of "80,000 people out of employment in New York this winter", he fails to recognise his predicament reflected in the news. His reaction – "What an awful thing that is" – is a response to something that seems to be going on elsewhere, even though he himself is out of work, apart from a brief spell as a scab in the streetcar strike. It's happening to him, too, but "What an awful thing that is" is all he can formulate by way of analysis. As for his own role in his personal tragedy, that doesn't even enter his cogitations.

"Dreiser's characters are low in the sense of being stupid," says Ellen Moers, the pioneering feminist critic and biographer of Dreiser. "Carrie... would probably rank well below the norm in any verbal intelligence test. Neither sentimentality nor disgust mars Dreiser's handling of inarticulate people."

"Tell the truth" was Dreiser's own motto for his writing, and he did. This is Dreiser's genius, his original achievement: not only in recognising (against the prevailing religious and even literary propaganda) that in real life women are often happier and more fulfilled when "fallen" than un-fallen, but also in giving a voice to the yearnings and even finer feelings of people largely ignored by the conventional novel, where everyone seems so self-aware.

Dreiser's plots not only took up and paid attention to the inarticulate people usually ignored by the writers of more conventional fiction, but also imagined feelings for them, however clumsily expressed. Which is to say that his version of naturalism went well beyond the material. "Dreiser's central theme in *Sister Carrie*," says Donald Pizer, "sets forth the idea – Lionel Trilling to the contrary – that the physically real is not the only reality and that men seek something in life beyond it."

My Ántonia

Ten-year-old Jim Burden, an orphan from Virginia, is sent to live with his grandparents in Black Hawk, Nebraska. They are farmers, but the area has recently been opened to homesteading – that is, government sponsored free settlement. As it happens, on the same train taking Jim to his grandparents are the Shimerdas, a family of homesteaders from Bohemia, in what is now the Czech Republic.

Jim becomes friends with the Shimerdas' oldest daughter, Ántonia. He teaches her English, while she helps out in his grandmother's kitchen. But the Shimerdas find it very hard on the homestead, breaking the sod for crops and living in a cave. Mr. Shimerda, homesick for Bohemia, kills himself before the first winter is out. The rest of the family struggle on, improving the farm and eventually building a frame house.

After a few years Jim's grandparents decide to rent their farm out and move to the edge of town. A neighbour needing a housekeeper to help out with the chores and look after the children hires Ántonia, who takes happily to town life, and starts to see Jim again. Jim does well in high school, eventually going to The University of Nebraska at Lincoln, where he studies classics. There he picks up again with another of the immigrant girls, Lena Lingard, whom he takes to dances and the theatre.

When Jim's classics teacher leaves for Harvard, Jim decides to follow him. Meanwhile, Ántonia gets engaged and moves to Denver, where her fiancé abandons her shortly before the wedding, leaving her pregnant. Despite her family's disapproval, Ántonia moves back home to look after her baby and help out on the farm.

Back from Harvard and about to enter law school, Jim visits Ántonia and spends a happy day catching up. Despite promising to visit again soon, he doesn't see her for 20 more years, by which time he is living in New York, unhappily married and working as an

Willa Cather's childhood home in Red Cloud, Nebraska

attorney for a big railroad, and she is happily married and settled on her own farm with ten more children.

My Ántonia could hardly be more different from *Huckleberry Finn*. That was a man's book about a boy lighting out from civilisation. Willa Cather had a very different take on the West from the standard male one, which imagined it as a place of escape. And far from winning the support of the white males of the critical world, *My Ántonia* is not even mentioned by Chase or Fiedler.

Some white males *have* paid attention to Cather, though not always approvingly. The British scholar and critic David Daiches, apparently expecting a sort of frontier re-run of *Middlemarch*, notes that "the central theme is... the development and self discovery of the heroine", yet because of the way the narrative is set up through Jim Burden, the reader

35

loses sight of Ántonia over large tracts of the book.

Blanche Gelfant agrees that the problem lies with Jim, not because he distracts us from Ántonia but because he fails to sleep with her – or with Lena or anyone else. "His flight from sexuality parallels a flight from historical truth," she writes, and this makes him an unreliable narrator.

Part of the problem comes from a misunderstanding of what kind of book this is. It is not a novel in the English sense; there is no development of character as such and not much of a plot, more a series of episodes. Furthermore, Jim's role is not to engage but to observe, to remember, to record. But this is no simple story of "lighting out" in an exhilarating escape from civilization. Both Cather and her narrator moved while they were young from Virginia to Nebraska, where the immense scale of sky and rolling prairie enlarged their sensibilities forever, yet their ultimate trajectory was from west to east, to New York City, where both spent their adult lives.

By contrast, the Bohemian immigrants are in Nebraska to stay, not on a romantic idyll but as an existential necessity. They live there year round, through freezing winter and blazing summer, trying to raise livestock, grow crops, and build houses, then towns and communities.

In other words, far from trying to break from their past, they retain a complex relationship with it, depending on which generation they belong to: the first homesick for it to the point of despair and even (in the case of Ántonia's father) suicide, the second suppressing the past in the process of building their new life, and the third reinventing it in an American context, like Ántonia's boy Leo, who picks up old Mr Shimerda's long abandoned violin to teach himself how to play.

Which probably explains why *My Ántonia*, for all its attention to future prosperity – the immigrants' settlement of the frontier, their progress in respect of living arrangements from caves, to sod huts to airy frame houses, the gradual increase in planted acreage and livestock holdings (not to mention healthy families) – is so haunted by the past.

It is a past made up of several layers. There is personal memory, which always entails a sense of loss: nostalgia, homesickness, even despair. For the more educated Jim Burden, whose framing narrative is split into the years of his youth and of his later return to the region, nostalgia is expressed in the tag from Virgil's *Georgics*, "Optima dies... prima fugit": the best days are the first to flee.

The absence of established communities and traditional practice is really the absence of boundaries, whether social or physical. It is mirrored in the blankness of the land. When Jim arrives in early Nebraska from the more settled state of Virginia, he is struck by how little there is to see: "no fences, no creeks, no trees, no hills or fields". To soften this anxiety over emptiness he seizes on the farmhand Otto Fuchs's belief that the lines of sunflowers across the land had been planted by the

Mormons – themselves a self-marginalising people – on their way west, to leave a trail for their fellow religionists to follow. But Fuchs's knowledge seems less than scientific: "I believe that botanists do not confirm Fuchs's story, but insist that the sunflower was native to those plains," says Jim.

A similar trace of history appears in the form of a circular track worn in the ground, where the Indians used to ride. But to do what? Torture an enemy tied to the stake in the middle of the circle, as Jake and Otto think, or – Grandfather's view – just to exercise their horses? Once again, the evidence is ambiguous and the trace is very indistinct. Then, in "The Hired Girls", comes the Spanish sword unearthed by the river. Did the Spanish under Coronado really get as far north as Nebraska? The historians say no, but Ántonia has seen the artefact "with my own eyes" so "the teachers were wrong!" Not necessarily; a trapper or Indian could have found the sword further south and dropped or lost it in Nebraska.

What these examples show is how desperate the characters are to believe that history has somehow reached out to them and how, by a willed fancy, they invariably decide on the more optimistic interpretation. Even Jim decides to see the Indian pony tracks as "a good omen for the winter".

And immediately after the discussion about the sword they spy an amazing thing. As the sun sinks in the west, a plough is outlined exactly at the centre of its red disk. This is nothing less than the emblem –

the logo – of *My Ántonia*. On the most immediate level it suggests that the plough will guarantee their personal future, as indeed it does. More generally, through its association with tilling the land (*cultura* in Latin), it blazes the promise that human settlement left behind in the Old Country, will renew itself in the New World as the land is cultivated.

For Willa Cather and her framing narrator Jim Burden, this process is accelerated in their classical education, in which ancient knowledge jumps the gap from Rome to Nebraska in the time it takes for a frontier settler to get to college. Burden has two favourite quotations from Virgil: "Optima dies... prima fugit", expressing the book's nostalgia for the past, and "Primus ego in patriam mecum... deducam Musas". ("I will be the first to carry the muse into my country.")

"'Patria' here meant not a nation... but the little rural neighbourhood on the Mincio where the poet was born." As Burden goes on to explain, Virgil hoped to "bring the Muse... not to the capital, the *palatia Romana,* but to his own little 'country'; to his father's fields."

This is the medieval figure of *translatio studii*, the idea expressed by the late 12th-century poet Chrétien de Troyes, among others, that knowledge moved like the sun, from east to west – from Eden through Jerusalem, Babylon, Athens and Rome to France. The English philosopher George Berkeley (1685 – 1753) would extend this progress westwards in his "On the Prospect of Planting Arts and Learning in America". The poem was so popular there that the University of California, the westernmost plantation of American learning, used its author's surname for its home campus.

Virgil was a farmer, too, of course. Burden thinks *Georgics* is his greatest work, "where the pen was fitted to the matter as the plough is to the furrow". With this phrase, as with the emblem of the plough against the sun, Cather expresses the faith that the movement westwards is not a falling off, but a transferring and renewal of culture in all its meanings.

The Age of Innocence

The scene is fashionable New York in the 1870s. Young lawyer Newland Archer is about to marry May Welland, when he meets her cousin Countess Ellen Olenska, herself a New Yorker by birth, newly returned to escape an unhappy marriage in Europe. She takes up residence in a Bohemian part of town, and mixes with married men who amuse and interest her.

Assigned by his law firm to advise Ellen on her forthcoming divorce, but really to dissuade her from it because of the scandal it would bring upon her family, Newland gets to know her and becomes increasingly attracted by her beauty, candour and dislike of the stifling social conventions of New York.

But, out of duty and loyalty to the families' expectations, he marries May. The union is unhappy. He can't forget Ellen; he wants to make her his mistress. She reciprocates his love but her European experience has made her sensitive to the tawdriness and eventual tedium of such arrangements.

Suddenly, word gets around that Ellen is returning to Europe. Newland tells May that he has been thinking of touring Europe on his own in the next year, but she reveals she is pregnant. It is at this point that Newland realises everyone suspects the affair, "and that now the whole tribe had rallied about his wife on the tacit assumption that nobody knew anything" (Chapter 33).

Twenty-six years later, May dies and Newland accepts his grown-up son's invitation to sail to Europe. In Paris the young man remembers that his mother's cousin lives there, and asks Newman to accompany him on a visit to Ellen's flat. Newman tells his son to go up and present himself, while he waits below. After a while, he walks alone back to their hotel.

Richard Chase, who thought that the best American authors wrote romances, condemned Edith Wharton as a novelist of manners, and therefore "among the writers of second or third rank". Leslie Fiedler doesn't even mention her in his *Love and Death in the American Novel.* So for the great post-war formers of the American literary canon, she was something of an unperson. Yet *The Age of Innocence* is a remarkable novel, worthy of the closest attention – and not just because it was a stunning popular success, for which Edith Wharton became the first woman to win the Pulitzer Prize.

She was indeed a novelist of manners, for the same reason as her mentor Henry James. Her early immersion in Europe (aged four in her case) widened her horizons and led, inevitably, to her making comparisons between Europe and the United States.

For a society as over-regulated as New York in the 1870s, Europe was both a treat and a threat. Of course everyone had to have European dresses or books, and to have their hands "modelled in Rome by the great Ferrigiani" (Chapter Foud). Moreover, the van der Luydens' social impact is much strengthened by the set of George II silver plate, the "Lowestoft" porcelain and the Crown Derby china that they set before their guests (Chapter Eight).

On the other hand, Europe is seen as impossibly liberal in morals, if not risqué. Julius Beaufort, the man-about-town of uncertain origins, is widely despised for his "vulgarity" and new money. But what really unnerves New York society is his cultural hybridity, his relaxed mastery of European conventions as well as American, "his habit of two continents and two societies, his familiar association with artists and actors and people generally in the world's eye, and his careless contempt for local prejudices" (Chapter 15). Of course this is precisely what attracts Ellen to him, and in turn makes New York society all the more suspicious of her.

'The Age of Innocence' by Joshua Reynold, believed to have been the inspiration for the title of Wharton's novel

As a result of these widened perspectives, the story is crammed with ironies, big and small. Arching over all is the problematic state of "innocence". There is about as much "innocence" in *The Age of Innocence* as there is mirth in Wharton's *The House of Mirth* (1905).* Early on in the book, while observing May from the Club box at the opera, Archer conceives a "tender reverence" for her

---

* The title for which was taken from the Book of Ecclesiastes, 7: 4: 'The heart of the wise [is] in the house of mourning, but the heart of fools [is] in the house of mirth.'

"abysmal purity".

The adjective is unconsciously apt, but the "purity" he imagines is, of course, sexual as much as intellectual. "She doesn't even guess what it's all about," thinks Newland – he means the "love interest" in the opera – and imagines that her education will commence when they "read *Faust* together... by the Italian lakes" on their honeymoon. Poor Newland: to imagine he can work on May's passions – or even ignite them in the first place – by sharing with her a German literary classic. It's he who gets the education, when he repeatedly underestimates her intuition and cunning.

In keeping with the close attention to detail necessary to a novel of manners, *The Age of Innocence* is a novel of surfaces. It is not only set *in* but is *about* a society that is itself entirely absorbed in display, in fashion, and in other surface tokens of a largely material world. Accordingly, the narrative follows the lead of the dominant characters, directing the reader's attention to what matters to them. All that attention to houses, furnishings, food and clothes mirrors their own preoccupation.

Sometimes the detailed description seems overdone in order to convey a sense of excess. After May wins the archery prize, she proposes visiting Granny Mingott's Newport house to tell the old lady in person of her triumph. Even the route is specified, and no proper name or technical term for a form of interior or exterior decoration is left out:

... she turned the ponies down Narragansett Avenue, crossing Spring Street and drove out toward the rocky moorland beyond. In this unfashionable region Catherine the Great... had built herself in her youth a many-peaked and cross-beamed *cottage-orné* on a bit of cheap land overlooking the bay. Here, in a thicket of stunted oaks, her verandahs spread themselves above the island-dotted waters. A winding drive led up between iron stags and blue glass balls embedded in mounds of geraniums to a front door of highly-varnished walnut under a striped verandah-roof; and behind it ran a narrow hall with a black and yellow star-patterned parquet floor, upon which opened four small square rooms with heavy flock-papers under ceilings on which an Italian house-painter had lavished all the divinities of Olympus. (Chapter 21)

The chief effect of all this is *weight*. Every noun ("oaks", "drive", "front door", "floor", "ceiling") is bowed down with its requisite, apparently inescapable, adjectival word or phrase – sometimes two or three of them. And explicitness too: we are allowed to imagine nothing for ourselves. Every square inch of the verbal canvas is covered; impressionistic it's not. Yet thus described, Granny Mingott's Newport "cottage" is a fair approximation to herself: not only to her excessive physical bulk but also her expansiveness of spirit and her general willingness to challenge convention. The house has all those qualities too.

As it happens, though, this emphasis on surface detail marks a significant departure from the more traditional novel of manners. Here the third-person narrative – it's almost a voice-over* – seems to be calling our attention to a sociological frame of reference, or even an anthropological one, as when it calls the final expulsion of the Countess Olenska in defence of May "a tribal rally around a kinswoman" (Chapter 33).

That repeated figure of the tribe was no random metaphor. Nancy Bentley has shown that for Wharton manners were not simply events to be chronicled in fiction, but observed as a science. *The Age of Innocence* represents what Bentley calls "a significant transformation of the traditional novel of manners":

> Retaining the drawing room settings and the portraits of sensibility of a Jane Austen novel, Wharton adds a subtext of crime, surveillance, and punishment more likely in a Dostoyevsky novel, or, more to the point, in a work like Bronislaw Malinowski's *Crime and Custom in Savage Society.*

The sense of detachment in the narrative is partly due to the time gap between when the novel was written and when it takes place. Its setting is

* It was indeed voiced – by Joanne Woodward – in Martin Scorsese's brilliant film of the novel (Columbia, 1993).

contemporaneous with that of *A Portrait of a Lady*, yet its composition came some 40 years later.

This distance in time is felt especially at the end. Archer is frozen in the street below Ellen's window in Paris, a relic, or museum exhibit of the old tribal order. Meanwhile, as Nancy Bentley puts it:

> Telephones and electric lighting, [Theodore] Roosevelt's politics, and rapid overseas travel have been integrated into the life of the next generation of leading New Yorkers. Even more important, the taboos against exogamous marriage to the sons and daughters of business and politics have been lifted. Now society is a "huge kaleidoscope where all the social atoms spun around on the same plane" (Chapter 34), but the disorder is an energy harnessed by Archer's children.

The Great Gatsby

The narrator of *The Great Gatsby* is Nick Carraway from Minnesota, a Yale graduate and World War One veteran, who comes east to learn the bond business in 1922. He settles in West Egg on the North Shore of Long Island, within commuting distance of New York, in "a weather-beaten cardboard bungalow" next door to an immense mansion inhabited by a mysterious man who gives a lot of elaborate parties.

Shortly after he arrives, Nick's cousin, Daisy Buchanan, asks him over for dinner in East Egg. Her husband, Tom, Nick had known at Yale. East Egg is where the "old money" have their mansions, as opposed to the "new money" parvenus of West Egg. Also present is Daisy's old friend, Jordan Baker, a champion golfer.

Tom has a mistress, Myrtle Wilson, wife of a garage owner in the "Valley of Ashes" between Long Island and New York City. He keeps a love nest for her in New York, to which Tom invites Nick so that he can meet her.

Finally an invitation arrives to one of those glittering parties next door. Jordan Baker is there, with whom Nick is beginning an affair. Nick meets the host, Jay Gatsby, who charms him with his friendliness and easy generosity, but like everyone else, Nick is mystified by his origins, his occupation and the source of his wealth.

Is he a bootlegger, a supplier of illicit alcohol during prohibition? He is always receiving urgent phone calls from out of state; is he at the heart of some nefarious financial scam? Is he really the son of a wealthy family from the Middle West, educated at Oxford? Jordan thinks he is lying, but then she is a cynical modern girl. So does Tom, but then Tom is a snob, as well being a bully, a racist and a serial adulterer. Nick doubts him too at first, especially

Opposite: The 1925 cover of The Great Gatsby

The GREAT GATSBY

F·SCOTT·FITZGERALD

when Gatsby identifies his middle-western home town as San Francisco (Chapter Four).

Some of Gatsby's mysteries are explained – sort of. He does come from the Midwest, but, as we learn much later, was a poor farm boy until he caught the attention of the mining magnate Dan Cody, from whom he learned to act rich, then to be rich. He did attend Trinity College, Oxford, on a brief visiting student arrangement offered to American Army officers after the war.

But the biggest puzzle is why he bought his North Shore mansion, across the bay from the Buchanans. The reason is Daisy. As a young officer he fell in love with her, but when he returned from Europe, she had married Tom. Gatsby's display of wealth, his legendary parties, are all an attempt to attract Daisy's attention.

Failing to attract her by his elaborate display, Gatsby persuades Nick to ask Daisy to tea without telling her that he'll be there too. The two lovers meet again, and start an affair. In time Tom begins to suspect the liaison, and finally stages a showdown. One hot afternoon he suggests they all drive into New York. At a loose end, they take a suite in the Plaza Hotel, where Tom turns on "Mr Nobody from Nowhere" for "making love" to his wife. Gatsby says Daisy has always loved him, never Tom. At first she confirms this claim, but after Tom suggests that Gatsby is involved in organised crime, and promises to take better care of her in the future, she ceases to resist him.

Driving back from New York in Gatsby's car, with Daisy at the wheel, they hit and kill Tom's mistress, Myrtle, outside the garage in the Valley of Ashes. Gatsby takes the blame. Recognising the car, George Wilson tracks Gatsby down and shoots him, then turns the gun on himself.

Daisy and Tom close ranks, and take off for an undisclosed address. After Gatsby's truncated funeral, attended only by himself and a handful of others, Nick returns to his home in the Midwest.

For a book that has become something of pin-up for American literature, *The Great Gatsby* did not do well when it came out in 1925. Whereas Fitzgerald's first two novels, *This Side of Paradise* (1920) and *The Beautiful and the Damned* (1922) had sold over 50,000 copies each, *Gatsby* weighed in at a disappointing 21,000 in the first year. "F. SCOTT FITZGERALD'S LATEST A DUD", said a now infamous headline in the *New York World*. The satirist and cultural critic F. L. Mencken wrote in the *Chicago Tribune* that it was "no more than a glorified anecdote". Ralph Coghlan, legendary fire-eating editor of the Saint Louis *Post-Dispatch*, opined that "its author seems a bit bored and tired and cynical. There is no ebullience here..."

In private Fitzgerald's fellow authors were more supportive – none more so than the modernist poet T. S. Eliot, who wrote to say the novel had "interested and excited me more than any new novel I have seen, either English or American, for a number of years... In fact it seems to me to be the first step that

American fiction has taken since Henry James."

It wasn't until World War II, when the Council on Books in Wartime ordered 155,000 paperback copies for distribution to American troops that *Gatsby* finally reached its deserved mass readership. By that time critical opinion had also had second thoughts, and today the book still sells half a million copies every year.

Even after the Second World War, however, those two canon formers, Richard Chase and Leslie Fiedler, remained unconvinced. Chase dismissed Fitzgerald as yet another purveyor of the novel of manners; Fiedler attacked *The Great Gatsby*'s febrile romanticising of sexuality. Daisy was "the first notable anti-virgin of our fiction", he said. She was "the White Bride turned Dark Destroyer".

> For Fitzgerald, 'love' was essentially yearning and frustration; and there is consequentially little genital love in his work, though he identified himself with that sexual revolution which the 20s thought of as their special subject.

Another early academic critic, Marius Bewley, argued that *The Great Gatsby* lamented the collapse of the American dream. This was a theme much taken up by subsequent commentators. Bewley was right, though not in the sense he meant. For him the American dream was nothing more than a belief in the "goodness of nature and man".

The real American dream was first elaborated by

Captain John Smith in his *A Description of New England* (1616). To promote New World settlement, Smith offered not gold and silver and an endless supply of slave labour (the usual inducements of the time), but the chance for poor and disadvantaged people in the Old World to earn an independent livelihood in the New, and to accumulate property that they could pass on to their children.

So to see the American dream as a general hope that things will get better, as so many commentators have done, is not quite right. Smith was thinking about class: how ordinary people without family money, or property, or even a fixed abode, could make and keep a fortune, a house, a legacy – how they could join the middle classes, or even become landed aristocrats in time.

In this sense, the American dream is certainly one theme of *The Great Gatsby.* The book is much preoccupied with class. Gatsby comes East from the Midwest to make good. So does Nick. When he drives over to dinner with the Buchanans in "fashionable East Egg", Nick thinks he has at last arrived at the social and cultural apex of American life.

His host is so rich that he can afford to keep a string of polo ponies. The Buchanans' lawn "started at the beach and ran toward the front door for over half a mile". Inside the house, the breeze "blew curtains in at one end and out the other like pale flags", while two women dressed in white on a couch, so apparently without the baser cares of the lower classes, seem to float "as though upon an anchored balloon".

But then something jars. "I've got a nice place here,' [Tom] said, his eyes flashing about restlessly." For all his wealth and strength, Tom is ill at ease. He is a bigot, ranting on about *The Rise of the Colored Empires*, and neither as secure, cultured or sophisticated as his immense wealth would suggest. Then he shuts the rear windows "with a boom", and "the curtains and the rugs and the two young women ballooned slowly to the floor". It's a remarkably powerful passage, a mime, or dumb-show of the plot to follow.

"I see now that this has been a story of the West, after all," says Nick, towards the end of the novel. "Tom and Gatsby, Daisy and Jordan and I, were all Westerners, and perhaps we possessed some deficiency in common which made us subtly unadaptable to the East."

This inability to fit into the East is first expressed in class terms, with Gatsby's pretensions to the settled status of old money. Tom is unable to fill the role of wealthy, cultured host, and Nick has social ambitions of his own (which, of course, undermine his attempt to keep an ironic distance as narrator).

But as westerners they are all "unadaptable" in an ethical sense, too, since they represent western "innocence", as opposed to the corruption of the over-civilised East. Except that they don't. None of these characters can be described as "innocent", though Gatsby, maybe, with the purity of his dream, however misdirected, could just about fit into the

F. Scott Fitzgerald in 1921

stereotype of the western *naif*. Daisy and Tom are far from innocent, as Nick finally comes to realise: "They were worthless people... they smashed up things and then retreated back into their money... and let other people clean up the mess they had made." Even Jordan cheats at golf.

One thing the men in the novel have in common is that they are all dreamers. Is that what makes them western? Or is it the peculiar nature of their dreams? For their dreams are all regressive. Determined to repeat the past ("Can't repeat the past?... Why of course you can!" (Chapter Six)), Gatsby wants to return Daisy to the 18-year old southern belle from Louisville, Kentucky, as she was when he first courted her. Nick dreams of his boyhood and young adulthood *returning* to the West on holiday: those vast fields of fresh snow ("*Our* snow"), those houses known by the names of the people who inhabited them for generations (Chapter Nine). Even Tom, the Yale football star, "one of those men who reach such an acute limited excellence at twenty-one that everything afterwards savours of anti-climax", is "forever seeking, a little wistfully, for the dramatic turbulence of some irrecoverable football game" (Chapter One).

The novel, or Nick's story, concludes with another dream, this time invoking the irrecoverable past of the whole nation, that famous unmaking of the history of American settlement in which the "inessential houses" seem to melt away until:

> I became aware of the old island here that flowered once for Dutch sailors' eyes – a fresh, green breast of the new world... for a transitory enchanted moment man must have held his breath in the presence of this continent, compelled into an aesthetic contemplation he neither understood nor desired, face to face for the last time in history with something commensurate to his capacity for wonder. (Chapter Nine)

And so we return to the first frontier of Captain John Smith, the vast continent opening itself to his conquest, except that now the dream has turned into the nightmare rape of the continent. So Nick's regressive dream of the frontier is always eaten up by the advance of Huck Finn's "sivilization". The tragedy of *The Great Gatsby* is that the progressive American dream has been destroyed by history, as, perhaps, are all dreams.

A Farewell to Arms

Frederic Henry is an American ambulance driver in the Italian Army during World War One. Catherine Barkley is a Scottish nurse in the unit. They begin a dalliance, which gradually matures into an affair. Frederic is wounded in the knee by a mortar shell, and is sent to a hospital in Milan. By chance Catherine is also transferred to Milan, and, as she looks after him, their love matures and deepens.

With the wound finally healed, Frederic is offered leave, but when he is discovered to have been drinking in the hospital he is sent back to the front, leaving Catherine three months pregnant. In the chaotic Italian retreat from the Austrian onslaught at Caporetto, Frederic's unit gets bogged down in the mud, and they finally have to disperse, abandoning their ambulances. Frederic is captured and questioned by the "battle police", who are shooting the retreating officers as traitors, but manages to escape by swimming away down a river. Figuring that his obligation to the war is over, he heads for Milan to find Catherine, only to hear that she has been transferred to Stresa on Lake Maggiore.

They spend time quietly together in Stresa, until they hear a rumour that he is about to be arrested for desertion. They decide to try to get to neutral Switzerland by rowing up the lake at night in the middle of a thunderstorm, finally reaching the shore the next day. After a delay, the Swiss allow them to stay. There they live quietly in the mountains until, when Catherine's baby is due, they move to Lausanne. The birth is difficult; the baby is still-born, then Catherine haemorrhages and dies. Frederic walks back through the rain to the hotel.

A Farewell to Arms was Ernest Hemingway's second novel, and by far his most popular. It was a bestseller, and has attracted a wide array of critical responses. Issues have been raised about various dualities, such as the two stories (is the novel about love or war?), the two narrators (Frederic Henry and Hemingway, so correspondingly two points of view), two Catherines (victim and heroine). There is even a plausible Lacanian analysis* by Ben Stolzfus: "In writing the story of his love for

---

* After Jacques Lacan (1901 – 1981), the French psychoanalyst renown for his Freudian readings of literature. In Lacanian theory the moment when toddlers first recognise themselves in a mirror is the moment they first become aware of themselves as individuals.

Catherine, Frederic is also recovering the wholeness and the unity of the pre-mirror phase."

Early critics tended to agree with Robert Penn Warren's introduction to the 1949 edition of the book that it was about the men and women who, confronting the terrible waste of World War One, had lost their moral and spiritual bearings and were forced to invent their own code of behaviour from scratch. This reading tapped into the myth of the "lost generation", a phrase first applied by a garage owner to his mechanic for not repairing Gertrude Stein's car on time, then related by Stein to Hemingway, who liked the glamour of the concept so much he used it as one of the epigraphs to his first novel *The Sun Also Rises* (1928).

Leslie Fiedler, however, wasn't having anything as romantically self-pitying as a lost generation. For him the lovers were simply escaping reality. "Poor things, all they wanted was innocent orgasm after orgasm on an island of peace in a world at war, love-making without end in a scarcely real country to which neither owed life or allegiance." But it couldn't last since, according to Fiedler, Hemingway, like most American writers, couldn't deal imaginatively with ordinary married love. "Only the dead woman becomes neither a bore nor a mother; and before Catherine can quite become either she must die, killed not by Hemingway, of course, but by childbirth! It is all quite sad and lovely at the end: the last kiss bestowed on what was a woman and is now a statue, the walk home through the rain."

But Fiedler's wasn't the last word on Catherine – far from it. Philip Young and Carlos Baker, see her as "idealized beyond the fondest wishes of most people"; Leo Gurko and Richard Hovey think she is so self-effacingly in love with Frederic Henry that it saps his will to live; Judith Fetterley takes the feminist view that Frederic goes out of his way to absolve himself from her death, leaving the reader with the conclusion that the only good woman is a dead one.

Sandra Spanier has a more nuanced view. She argues that during the course of the story Frederic evolves from a callow youth into a mature man capable of confronting the full truth of his situation, while Catherine "plays a vital role in bringing about that developing awareness". She does this through the perspective of having lost her fiancé in the Battle of the Somme, and with him, her "faith in traditional values". So "Catherine has come to the relationship painfully wiser to the world than is the young man who happens into the war thinking it has nothing to do with him".

She "educates" him, says Spanier, through a series of small ironic corrections to his cynicism, or indifference, or occasional bursts of romantic ignorance, as when he proclaims that "'the coward dies a thousand deaths, the brave but one'", and she counters: "The brave dies perhaps two thousand

deaths, if he's intelligent. He simply doesn't mention them." Spanier is surely right to note that "Catherine's mode of ironic understatement (she is British)... most often [has] been overlooked – her laconic style considered, if at all, as evidence of her underdeveloped character."

So much of the critical debate on *A Farewell to Arms* might almost be about real people in an actual conflict, almost as if the narrative style and strategy by which these characters are articulated can be ignored. But of course Hemingway's style is legendary, his own invention, what set him off from other authors of his time. What was it? How did it work?

It can best be described as *subtractive*; it works by cutting out the superfluous. In Paris, Hemingway had become friendly with the American poet Ezra Pound, seeking his help with his early prose studies. Pound was then in his imagist phase, characterised by his "In a Station of the Metro":

The apparition of these faces in the crowd;
Petals on a wet, black bough. (1913)

This poem itself was subtractive. Its first draft had been 33 lines long; it was reduced in stages over a year after the initial experience until only the primary image was left.

Pound encouraged Hemingway to distrust adjectives, and to work toward a compressed style, short on explicit explanations. Hemingway followed the advice, reducing the number not only of adjectives, but also of adjectival (and adverbial) phrases and clauses, relying on simple declarative sentences, often conjoined by "and" or "but". The result was his famous "flat" style: concrete, descriptive, short on analysis or opinion or "editorial content" – like good journalism.

Hemingway picked up from Pound the literary device of mentioning someone as though he or she has already been introduced. Pound does it in his "Metro" poem ("*these* faces" – what faces?); Hemingway does it in *The Sun Also Rises*, where he introduces a main character with the words: "...and with them was Brett". Who is Brett? We have to work it out.*

In the same way *A Farewell to Arms* starts with an unadorned description of an unnamed village in an unspecified year:

> In the late summer of that year we lived in a house in a village that looked across the river and the plain to the mountains. In the bed of the river there were pebbles and boulders, dry and white in the sun, and the water was clear and swiftly moving and blue in the channels. Troops went by the house and down the road and the dust they raised powdered the leaves of the trees.

* The first chapter of a late draft of the novel was a lengthy introduction, by way of a mini-biography of Brett Ashley, but Hemingway cut it out at a late stage, after criticism from Fitzgerald.

Only with the last sentence does the war begin to make its way obliquely into the story. Yet the particulars of the river and pebbles and sun and water – once again designated with definite articles, as though we already knew them – have established the narrative priorities.

Yet the narrative voice cannot be simply flat and neutral, since it's Frederic's, and he has changed since Catherine's lessons in irony and proportion, and her death. It is obvious, though sometimes overlooked, that he has been through the experiences chronicled in the book before he starts to tell the story, so two levels of narrative voice are inevitable: one naive, simply recording, the other more knowing.

So only three paragraphs on from the beginning Frederic describes the soldiers trudging by in the rain, their cartridge belts swelling their capes as if they "were six months gone with child". His imagery suggests how far Frederic has swerved from neutrality even at the start of the book. And if first-time readers cannot yet grasp the significance of pregnancy in the rain, there's no missing the knowing irony ending that first chapter: "At the start of the winter came... the cholera. But it was checked and in the end only seven thousand died of it in the army."

And it's clear that in this book the deliberately flat tone is more than a characteristic style; it embodies a politics developed in reaction to a war in which abstract nouns like "glory, honour, courage...

were obscene beside the concrete names of villages, the numbers of roads the names of rivers, the numbers of regiments and the dates" (Chapter 27).

With the personal and tangible taking priority over the official, no wonder the moments of real suspense come in unexpected places. These aren't in the headline action of, say, the Italian defeat at Caporetto in the autumn of 1917, but in practical struggles like the ambulance drivers' efforts to get their heavy vehicles out of the mud during the long retreat from the rout, and Catherine's and Frederic's escape to Switzerland in a rowing boat during a rainstorm (Chapters 29 and 37).

Yet for all his laid-back tone, when Hemingway needs an urgent, excited, wholly subjective response on his narrator's part, he can produce it. Here is what takes over Frederic Henry's mind as his beloved Catherine dies of her multiple haemorrhages :

> I knew that she was going to die and I prayed that she would not. Don't let her die. Oh, God, please don't let her die. I'll do anything for you if you won't let her die. Please, please, please, Dear God, don't let her die. Dear God, her die. You took the baby but don't let her die - that was all right but don't let her die. Please, please, dear God, don't let her die (Chapter 41).

Only when she's gone, after he sits briefly with her body, does he revert to that flat affect-free mode of narration. Once again, as with all bad things in the novel, it takes place in the rain. Only now, after the frankness of emotion, the contrast is overwhelming:

> But after I had got them out and shut the door and turned off the light it wasn't any good. It was like saying good-bye to a statue, After a while I went out and left the hospital and walked back to the hotel in the rain.

The Sound and the Fury

Instead of a conventional story *The Sound and the Fury* gives us four reactions to a sequence of events, each taking place at a different time in the past, between 1898 and 1928. All four accounts are flawed, or partial. The first is, literally, the "tale told by an idiot" which the title implicitly refers to – the phrase comes from Macbeth's despairing reflection that life is "A tale told by an idiot,/Full of sound and fury/Signifying nothing" – and it is radically disorganised. The second is fixated obsessively on just one of these events, and the third is distorted by spite and self pity. The last doesn't refer to the historical occurrences specifically, but passes a magisterial comment on their role in the decline of the Compson family.

The elements of the past that so preoccupy the four narrators can be summarised as follows. In

William Cuthbert Faulkner (1897-1962)

1898, when the children are young, their grandmother dies; this news is kept from them. Her body is laid out in the parlour. Caddy climbs a tree to see what's going on. Before that she has been playing in the "branch"(stream) and got her knickers muddy; the three boys – Quentin, Jason and Benjy – see her dirty underwear when she climbs the tree.

Twelve years on Mr. Compson sells Benjy's meadow to raise the money to send Quentin to Harvard. Caddy becomes pregnant by Dalton Ames, then marries Herbert Head, a banker. Also in 1910, at the end of his first year at Harvard, Quentin, obsessed with Caddy's disgrace, kills himself by jumping into the Charles River.

Herbert discovers that Caddy's baby wasn't his, leaves her and withdraws his offer to Jason of a job in his bank. Caddy is barred from the Compson house, but her illegitimate daughter, Quentin, is adopted by the family. By 1928, the year of the last two narratives, she is 18 years old.

For Richard Chase, Faulkner's work represented the best of American fiction to date. "The many-sided genius of Faulkner," he says, "has performed so far the greatest feat of twentieth-century American fiction." In *The Sound and the Fury* the "element of romance is completely assimilated and sublimated, so that it becomes a suffused poetry of language, metaphor and event".

Leslie Fiedler, on the other hand, thought Faulkner's work typical of that kind of American imaginative writing he most deplored, in that it was "bewilderingly and embarrassingly, a gothic fiction, nonrealistic and negative, sadist and melodramatic – a literature of darkness and the grotesque in a land of light and affirmation".

By "land of light and affirmation", Fiedler may have meant the United States as a whole, but many – and especially William Faulkner – would withhold that encomium from the old Confederate South, which had been in cultural and economic eclipse since the end of the Civil War (1861 – 1865). And if anything, Faulkner's fiction sidesteps that old American division between romance and (realistic) novel; adjectives like "tragic" and "epic" would come closer to describing his multi-volume narrative of the South's post-war decline, through the fortunes of three families, the aristocratic Compsons and Sartorises, and the rapacious redneck Snopeses.

Of the four narratives in *The Sound and the Fury*, undoubtedly the most challenging is the first, Benjy's, told by a 33-year-old man with the mind of a three-year-old child. Benjy Compson's chapter is also the purest stream of consciousness,* being wholly self-enclosed, dipping unpredictably into various moments in the past, without self awareness or analysis. His jumps in time are random and unconscious, though usually pivot on a concrete sense impression, like a smell, a sound, the sight of something. Faulkner provided italics to give a sense (but only an approximate one) of where the time jumps come.

If Benjy's narrative has no sense of time or analysis, Quentin's has an excess of both. But the difference between his and Benjy's time shifts is that he recognises them as such – as memories, like his classical and (more frequent) Biblical allusions.

After this strenuous, adolescent, contradictory and self-destructive discourse, Jason's narrative comes as a relief. In his "Appendix" written 16 years

* That is, not only unmediated by an external narrator, but unshaped and untrimmed even by the person in whose mind the thoughts and feelings occur. The device was first used by the Irish modernist James Joyce (1882 – 1941) for the voice of Molly Bloom in his novel *Ulysses* (1929).

after the book came out, Faulkner called Jason "the only sane Compson since Culloden".* Donald Kartiganer wonders "how anyone, especially Faulkner, could have considered Jason sane or rational", since "he is in fact far less aware of what is actually real than his brother Quentin". It's true, too, that Jason's suppression of all feeling in favour of profit and loss – while totally misconstruing *real* profit and loss, even in monetary terms – cuts him off from his family, not to mention the rest of humanity, as much as Benjy and Quentin.

But the point is not whether Jason is sane or mad, or even likeable (he's not). What is important is his role in the narrative. His voice is the first with a trace of humour. It may be humour that is mainly destructive of other people's pretensions and illusions, and often mere sarcasm, as when he remarks to Miss Quinton playing hooky in her kimono: "I reckon that's your school costume, is it?... Or maybe today's a holiday."

Still, a sense of humour, however racist, misogynistic and generally malignant, entails a sense of proportion. So Jason's narrative is another stage in the widening of perspective on the Compson family saga. And at this point in the novel some destruction of pretensions is surely called for, if only to relieve the claustrophobia.

So Jason's sarcasm is an apt response to his

* The Battle of Culloden, 1746, in which the Scots Jacobites (followers of Charles Edward Stuart) were finally defeated by the Hanoverian forces under the Duke of Cumberland.

mother's self-pitying snobbery:

> "Good Lord," I says. "You've got a fine mind. No
> wonder you keep yourself sick all the time."
> "What?" she says, "I don't understand."

No, she doesn't. Heritage, blood lines, family tradition and honour, the great positions filled by Compsons down the years of the southern past – all are at a discount now: "Blood, I says, governors and generals. It's a damn good thing we never had any kings and presidents; we'd all be down there at Jackson chasing butterflies." (Jackson is the state Asylum for the Insane, where he itches to send Bentley.)

The final chapter is the least "experimental" of the novel, being a conventional third-person narrative, getting into no one's head, but instead limited to what an observer would see and hear. It is centred on Dilsey, but Faulkner either couldn't or wouldn't put it in her voice.

As a third-person account, it achieves a degree of objectivity. This is the first place in the novel where the reader gets a view of Benjy from the outside, as though he had yet to be introduced: "a big man who appeared to have been shaped of some substance whose particles would not or did not cohere to one another or to the frame which supported it".

Near the beginning comes a remarkable paragraph describing, in detailed stages, how Dilsey fetches wood from the outdoor woodpile while coping with an open umbrella in the wind, stacks the wood in her arms, picks up the umbrella and tries to re-open it, then returning to the steps into the kitchen.

You might call this slow prose. As it unwinds it shows how painfully and painstakingly Dilsey works to get the house moving. Here the perspective widens further. This is what has been going on behind the scenes all along, while Mrs Compson demands her hot water bottle knowing that Dilsey has painfully to mount the stairs one step at a time to deliver it to her, while Miss Quentin bargains for another cup of coffee before playing hooky from school, while Jason complains of having "to work ten hours a day to support a kitchen full of niggers in the style they're accustomed to" and then reacts furiously the one night when it hasn't been possible to prepare him a hot dinner.

"That's the trouble with nigger servants," says Jason, "when they've been with you for a long time they get so full of self importance that they're not worth a dam. Think they run the whole family."

But that's just what Dilsey does. She has been doing every material thing that keeps the household going. And it's she who has the only true perspective on the Compsons' decline – true, that is, because it is not infected with self-pity or false pride or a neurotic fixation on a woman's honour.

It comes to her when she hears the Reverend Shegog's sermon. Significantly his voice modulates from white to black as his discourse proceeds –

"they did not mark just when his intonation, his pronunciation, became negroid" – but the theme his black voice proclaims is the true prophecy: "I sees the darkness en de death everlastin upon de generations."

Dilsey embarrasses her daughter Frony with her unstoppable tears. "'Whyn't you quit dat, mammy?... Wid all dese people lookin. We be passin white folks soon.'"

"I've seed de first and de last," Dilsey said, "never you mind me." [She is quoting Revelations 22.13: "I am Alpha and Omega, the beginning and the end, the first and the last."]

"First en last what?" Frony said.

"Never you mind," Dilsey said. "I seed de beginning, en now I sees de endin."

The Grapes of Wrath

By its peak in 1933, the Great Depression in the United States had resulted in more than 100,000 business failures, farm income cut in half, the failure of 5,000 banks, and 13 million men and women, more than 20% of the workforce, out of a job.

But the abiding image we have of the depression today is its effect on rural America. In popular memory, an extreme drought coincided with the economic downturn to turn most of the West into a "dustbowl", forcing tens of thousands of farmers in Texas, Arkansas and Oklahoma to up stakes and drive west to find work in California.

That's the story. The truth is rather different. Although the drought was real enough, the dust storms brushed past Oklahoma and Texas only at the two panhandles where the states meet, and missed Arkansas by 400 miles. In any case the migration from the south-western states to the West Coast was not restricted to displaced tenant farmers, and had been under way since before World War One. More migrants arrived in California between 1910 and 1930 than during the whole of the depression.

But it is the popular story that John Steinbeck drew on in his two Depression novels, *In Dubious Battle* (1936) and *The Grapes of Wrath* (1939). And given how timely it was when they came out, it is unsurprising that early reviews of both paid less attention to their literary merits than to their likely effect on American society. Would they help the working man?

No, thought Mary McCarthy. *In Dubious Battle* was full of "long and frequently pompous verbal exchanges". Steinbeck was a natural storyteller but he was "no philosopher, sociologist, or strike tactician". Steinbeck himself was furious about her brief (one page) review, as was his biographer, Jackson Benson, who labelled McCarthy "one of those parlor theoreticians who never get [their] hands dirty".

John Steinbeck pictured during his trip to Sweden to accept the Nobel Prize for Literature in 1962

But McCarthy was right. Steinbeck built *In Dubious Battle* around a peach strike on the Tagus Ranch in Visalia, California in 1933, a struggle famously won by the workers. To find out how they succeeded, the novelist interviewed, among others, the strike's organisers, yet when he incorporated the strike into the novel he had them all lose, through bad organisation, bitter infighting between the workers and union officials, lack of food and funds.

Why did he ignore his own research into the Tagus Ranch strike? Because he wanted the book to illustrate a theory to which he had become much attached, the so-called "phalanx theory" which held that human beings are deprived of personal choice when the individual becomes part of a group. In swallowing this fashionable nonsense it was Steinbeck, not McCarthy, who was the parlour theoretician.

The Grapes of Wrath, however, was different. This time Steinbeck visited one of the government camps set up for farm migrants and got to know how the organisers welcomed the itinerant workers, made them feel secure, encouraged them to manage their daily lives, helped with labour disputes and other relationships with the local community, and kept the growers' vigilantes from bullying the workers. Following his research, Steinbeck wrote a series of articles for the *San Francisco News,* contrasting the migrants' predicament in makeshift squatters' camps along the roads and drainage ditches with their lives in the government camps.

The epic sweep of *The Grapes of Wrath* – and its close attention to the tragedy of the Joad family as they moved westward in search of work – convinced contemporary critics that here at last was a book to promote a radical change in American society. "If only a couple of million overcomfortable people can be brought to read it," said Clifton Fadiman in *The New Yorker* in April 1939, "John Steinbeck's 'The Grapes of Wrath' may actually effect something like a revolution in their minds and hearts." Although many critics will be "ohing and ahing about Steinbeck's impressive literary qualities", this book is really "a social novel exposing social injustice".

The story traces the progress of Ma and Pa Joad, their parents and children, three generations of tenant farmers, forced off their land in Oklahoma when the bank forecloses on their loan, making their way along Highway 66 to California, where rumour and deceitful advertising promise farm jobs galore available. They are joined by their son Tom and Jim Casy, a former preacher. On the way first Granpa dies, then Granma. Connie, husband of their pregnant daughter Rose of Sharon, lights out soon after they get to California.

Because so many migrants have made their way west, work in California turns out to be much scarcer, and wages much lower, than advertised. The Joads struggle to live on their meagre earnings, until they land in Weedpatch, one of the migrant camps set up by the government. Here they are treated with respect, are given access to dry bedding, toilets and washing facilities, and make friends with other campers. They admire the migrants' self government, and appreciate the camp's immunity from sheriff's deputies and vigilantes.

But not even the farms around Weedpatch provide enough work to live on, so the Joads have to move on. They work as strike-breakers on a peach farm. Casy becomes a union organiser, and is killed when a vigilante crushes his skull with a pick handle. Tom seizes the weapon and uses it to kill the assailant. He lights out, promising his mother to be there to fight "wherever they's a fight so hungry people can eat... wherever they's a cop beatin' up a guy".

With the family now reduced to Ma, Pa, Rose of Sharon and the young ones, Ruthie and Winfield, the Joads move to an old boxcar (or goods van, as the British would call it) in a makeshift migrant camp. Rose of Sharon's baby is stillborn. When their boxcar is flooded out, they make for a barn on higher ground where they encounter a boy and a starving old man. To save his life Rose of Sharon offers him her breast.

One of the innovations that marked the book off from Steinbeck's earlier work were the 29 factual chapters woven into the fiction of the Joads' story, ranging in topic from the dust storms that start the whole migrant process off, to the heavy rains at the end of the novel. Each seeks to capture a specific set of events in the migrants' experience. This one brings alive the anxieties amounting almost to terror involved in keeping an overloaded old car moving along Route 66:

Listen to the motor. Listen to the wheels. Listen with your ears and with your hand on the steering wheel; listen with the palm of your hand on the gearshift lever; listen with your feet on the floor boards. Listen to the pounding old jalopy with all your senses, for a change of tone, a variation of rhythm may mean – a week here? That's tappets. Don't hurt a bit. Tappets can rattle till Jesus comes again without no harm. But that thudding as the car moves along – can't hear that – just kind of feel it. Maybe oil isn't gettin' someplace.

A still from the 1940 film adaptation of The Grapes of Wrath, *starring Henry Fonda*

Maybe a bearing's startin' to go. Jesus, if it's a bearing, what'll we do? Money's going fast.

Drawing on Steinbeck's proven and powerful journalistic skills, these factual interpolations promote the Joad story to almost epic dimensions. They certainly contributed to the book's early reputation, to its high sales (2,500 copies *a day* sold in May 1939; 14,600,000 paperbacks sold by 1982), to the book's Pulitzer Prize in 1939, and ultimately to Steinbeck's award of the Nobel Prize for Literature in 1962.

By this time critics were paying more attention to its literary qualities. Much was made of the archetypes on which it seemed to draw, like the mythical American attraction to the western frontier, or the even more universal Biblical epic of the Jews' escape from Egyptian captivity and Exodus to the Promised Land. Casy, of course, was seen as a "Christ figure". "Steinbeck's best work," said the Californian critic and historian David Wyatt, "naturalizes in his home state the central Western legend of... settlement, corruption, fall, and eviction. *The Grapes of Wrath* is the last of these, and California is the garden lost."

But even the book's admirers have had trouble with its ending. "The first three quarters [of it] are masterful," says Howard Levant, with the "characters presented through action" and the central theme dramatised in "a solid, realised documentary context". But towards the end, "characters are fitted or forced into allegorical roles" and "scenes are developed almost solely as links in an allegorical pattern".

Clifton Fadiman, among the first to proclaim the book as likely to provoke an epoch-making change in the American consciousness, could not stomach the ending either:

> Casy, the ex-preacher, is half real, half "poetic" in the worst sense of the word. Occasionally the folk note is forced a little. And, finally, the ending (a young girl who has only a day or two before given birth to a dead child offers the milk of her breasts to a starving man) is the tawdriest kind of fake symbolism.

What these astute critics are complaining of is

(oddly) that *The Grapes of Wrath* turns over-literary at the end. There is something else about the ending which strikes a false note. Although Steinbeck was enthusiastic about the government camp for migrants, Weedpatch, in his journalism, his story has the Joads forced to move on from it after only a month. It is Ma who insists they up stakes. Pa demurs: "'This here hot water an' toilets', Pa began. 'Well we can't eat no toilets.'" They're out of work, so have to move on.

Yet while the demand for labour certainly fell off in winter there would still have been work to be had at Weedpatch, as Steinbeck knew: pruning and spraying grapevines, burning bush, ditching, picking olives. And while, by the end of February, many would have remained unemployed, and would have had to receive help from the "good neighbors" in the camp, no one would have been destitute, or forced to leave instead of eating toilets.

Why did Steinbeck make things turn out worse for his fictional family than for migrants in the real government farm-migrant camp? Because the Joads' stay in Weedpatch is only a stage in a longer trajectory, from the dust storms in Oklahoma to the barn in which they are forced to take refuge by the floods after Rose of Sharon loses her baby. And in Steinbeck's story that trajectory is unrelievedly downward. As they work their way west, one after another of the extended family is stripped away, as first Granpa and then Granma die, Connie and Noah the preacher defect, and Tom goes into hiding.

Now reduced to its nucleus, the family is finally backed up against the wall of a barn, unable to move any further. They are even cut off from their future, as Rose of Sharon's baby is stillborn.

Authors often report that they have no idea how a novel is going to end until they get there. Not so Steinbeck. That ending, with the Joads finally made immobile, and Rose of Sharon's "symbolic" gesture (for that's the best it can be – a gesture) of offering her breast to the starving old man – all that was fixed in Steinbeck's head before he started the book. Like the phalanx theory in *In Dubious Battle*, it was there before the life of the novel began to stir and grow and unfold.

So that old California naturalism, or what Lionel Trilling called "American reality", won out in the end – a reality that was always hard, always unpleasant. Steinbeck, who prided himself on being a realist, his powers of realistic expression honed by journalism, sacrificed realism in the end to the idea, or literary convention, that nature always brings us down, however strongly our human solidarity, our well intended stratagems, our compassion and our imagination may try to fight it.

John Ford, who directed the superb 1940 film of the novel, wanted nothing to do with the breast-to-starving-man scenario. The movie ends with Ma and Pa Joad leaving the government camp, along with other families, not because they are starving but because it's time to move north in search of another seasonal crop, as so many farm migrants did. And so Ford returned Steinbeck's creation to the social novel, rooted in the documentary context so admired by the more discerning critics.

Native Son

Bigger Thomas, a 20-year-old African-American, wakes up in the squalid apartment he shares with his mother, sister and younger brother on the South Side of Chicago. A rat scampers across the floor. Bigger kills it with a frying pan.

Bigger has the chance of a job living with the Daltons – as their chauffeur. They are a wealthy white family, anxious to engage with what was then called the "Negro question", though Mr. Dalton has shares in the property company that owns the slums in which Bigger and his family live. On his first day at work the Daltons' daughter Mary asks Bigger to drive her to meet her communist boyfriend Jan. Trying to convince Bigger of their tolerant attitude towards Negros, Jan and Mary ask Bigger to call them by their first names, then to take them to "one of those places where colored people eat" on the South Side.

Later they drive around while Mary and Jan attack a bottle of rum in the back seat, and then make love. By the time Bigger drives Mary home, she is so drunk she can't get to her room unaided; so he has to carry her to bed. At this point Mary's mother comes in the room, and though blind, she can smell the alcohol on Mary's breath. Bigger, terrified that he'll be accused of seducing and raping Mary, tries to silence her by placing a pillow over her face, accidentally smothering her.

Now truly panicked beyond all reason, Bigger drags Mary's body down to the cellar to feed it into the furnace. He has to decapitate it in order to fit it in. The next day Bigger tells the Daltons that Mary had asked him to leave the car outside rather than put it in the garage, allowing them to suspect that Jan and she had run away after he had driven her home.

When Bigger tells his girlfriend Bessie what has happened, she is terrified, certain that he will be found out and – worse – suspected of having raped Mary before killing her. They run away, hiding in an abandoned building. They get drunk. Bigger rapes Bessie, then after she falls asleep crushes her head in with a brick, to keep her from talking. Meanwhile Mary's bones are discovered in the Dalton furnace.

Now on the run, Bigger faces the massed hostility of press and populace. After a gunfight he is captured. Jan comes to visit him in prison, even though he knows that Bigger tried to implicate him in Mary's disappearance. Jan introduces Bigger to a communist lawyer called Boris Max, who will defend him for no fee. Through long conversations with his lawyer Bigger begins to come to terms with his rage and incomprehension, seeing them in terms of his social condition. Despite Max's arguments in court, though, the local popular prejudice against black criminals is so strong as to make a guilty verdict a foregone conclusion, and Bigger is sentenced to die in the electric chair.

Most early reviews of *Native Son* were enthusiastic, interpreting Bigger's violence as the result of white prejudice and exploitation. Sales were buoyant: 215,000 copies in the first week, boosted by an early Book-of-the-Month Club selection.

A dissenting voice came from Burton Rascoe in *The American Mercury*, the literary journal founded (though at this point no longer owned) by the satirist and cultural critic, H.L. Mencken. Rascoe thought the book was so popular only because "these good people, the reviewers, go easily haywire about anything which looks to them like a social document exposing 'conditions'". Against "the hurrahing... I rise to assert that I think that the moral in *Native Son* is utterly loathsome and utterly insupportable as a message".

It wasn't just conservative white columnists who objected. The African-American novelist James Baldwin, though an admirer and indeed disciple of Richard Wright, thought that the impulse to protest interfered with the humane mission of the novel. "The failure of the protest novel lies in the rejection of life," he wrote.

Despite the book's early popularity with progressive-minded critics, and its high status among historians of African-American writing, there is a lot to be said for these objections. Granted Bigger suffers from a deprived childhood and a young manhood scarred by white prejudice, but Mary's murder and the rape and murder of Bessie – however much the blame may be mitigated by his racial marginality – risks (to put it mildly) losing the reader's sympathy.

Wright seems to have intended this alienation. Two years before *Native Son* came out, he had published a collection of five stories under the title of *Uncle Tom's Children*. Reviews were so positive that, as he writes in the Introduction to *Native Son*:

> I found that I had written a book which even bankers' daughters could read and weep over and feel good about. I swore to myself that if I wrote another book, no one would weep over it; that it would be so hard and deep that they would have to face it without the consolation of tears.

If Bigger is not a conventional novelistic character who matures as experience enhances his knowledge and feelings, he does develop in another way, in his command of voice. In fact the plot of *Native Son* is built around Bigger's voice.

Throughout the novel "there is but one point of view: Bigger's", says the author in his introduction. True, and yet for most of the story we hear very little of his *literal* voice, since he takes part in so little verbatim dialogue, contributing mainly the occasional "Yessah" or "Yessum". Until the end, Bigger is largely speechless, even when talking to

Richard Wright (1908 - 1960)

Mary and Jan, who offer their friendship and profess their equality with him: "You know, Bigger, I've long wanted to go into those houses," says Mary, pointing to the run-down tenements from which her father derives the exorbitant rent, "and just *see* how your people live... Never in my life have I been inside a Negro home. Yet they *must* live like we live. They're *human*..."

Without being able to articulate it, Bigger senses the naivety underlying Mary's genuine goodwill towards him, and more particularly how her grammar of "them" and "us" undercuts her expression of solidarity between the races. And when Jan professes his egalitarian feelings by forbidding Bigger from calling him *Sir* – "You're a man like I am; I'm no better than you. Maybe other white men like it. But I don't" – Bigger is rendered almost speechless: "'Ok,...' he mumbled, hoping that they did not hear the choke in his voice."

In these exchanges and others like them, he says little, but his voice comes out in long, fluent passages of free indirect style, reflecting the acute embarrassment amounting to aggression that he feels when confused by these whites who profess to mean him well:

> He flushed warm with anger. Goddam her soul to hell! Was she laughing at him? Were they making fun of him? What was it they wanted? Why didn't they leave him alone? He was not bothering them. Yes, anything could happen with people like these. His entire mind and body were painfully concentrated into a single sharp point of attention. He was trying desperately to understand.

Bigger's encounters with Mary and Jan are the most intensely imagined parts of the novel, because the reader's sympathies are wholly engaged with both parties in the debate: with the whites, who mean well, even if on the level of political theory more than felt emotion, and with Bigger, who is embarrassed and humiliated by their attempts to communicate.

So, in terms of voice, Bigger is the exact opposite of Dilsey in *The Sound and the Fury*. We can hear her voice, but we never get inside her head. Bigger can't speak aloud, but his perspective dominates *Native Son* from beginning to end.

Well, until almost the end. After his fear, his crime, his flight, his trial and his sentence to death, Bigger is somehow free to speak, analyse, reflect, articulate his feelings about what has happened. He has, literally, found his voice – on all levels. He can at last integrate what he's thinking with what he can say aloud. As John Reilly has put it, only Jan, who makes the "willed effort to understand Bigger, allows him the right to hate, and thus accepts the premise of the autobiography Bigger yearns to voice".

Max, his Communist lawyer, finds Bigger's new-found articulacy much harder to hear.

> "I ain't trying to forgive nobody [Bigger tells Max] and I ain't asking for nobody to forgive me. I ain't going to cry. They wouldn't let me live and I killed. Maybe it ain't fair to kill, and I reckon I really didn't want to kill. But when I think of why all the killing was, I began to feel what I wanted, what I am..."
>
> Bigger saw Max back away from him with compressed lips, but he felt he had to make Max understand how he saw things now.
> "I didn't want to kill!" Bigger shouted. "But what I killed for, I *am*! It must have been pretty deep in me to make me kill! I must have felt it awful hard to murder..."

Max lifted his hand to touch Bigger, but did not.

"No; no; no... Bigger, not that...," Max pleaded despairingly.

"What I killed for must have been good!" Bigger's voice was full of frenzied anguish. "It must have been good! When a man kills, it's for something... I didn't know I was really alive in this world until I felt things hard enough to kill for 'em."

There it all is, the black voice at last emancipated: free to speak, with no accent to set it off as a curious and harmless exhibit. Max, the communist, can't bear this "emancipation" because he believes in progress earned through the immersion of the ego in communal altruism, and Bigger's new-found credo – that personal power comes through violence – is closer to fascism than communism. Does the reader's reaction to Bigger follow Max's lead? Yes. Murder is a high price for his victims to pay to allow Bigger to feel free and speak freely about it.

Wright's deliberate attempt to alienate Bigger from the reader's affections suggests that he may have had the German communist playwright Bertolt Brecht (1898–1956) in mind, and specifically his noted theatrical device of what he called *Verfremdungseffekt*, or a distancing effect. Brecht would introduce elements into his dramas deliberately intended to discourage the audience from identifying too closely with the characters, in order to direct their attention to the underlying meaning of the play.

So, in *Mother Courage and her Children* (1939), which is about a civilian merchant who follows the Swedish army in her cart selling provisions to the troops during the Thirty Years War, audiences are prevented from identifying with the main character, who, though gritty, determined, cunning and sometimes brave, is also heartless. She refuses both to claim the body of her son, and to let the death of her daughter impede her relentless progress with the army.

Brecht's idea was that if the audience could be distanced from the personality of Mother Courage, they would concentrate more on the horrors of war that consume all who follow it, for whatever motive – heroic as well as mercenary. Richard Wright's distancing of Bigger is his way of not letting us forget the degree of alienation that (as he says in his introduction) "American oppression has fostered in him".

Conclusion

How did such an optimistic country, a society founded on so many progressive hopes for the future, come to produce so much sad fiction? There are plenty of unhappy endings in English novels during this period, of course, especially from the late 19th century onwards, when the sunny, relatively stable world of Jane Austen had given way to the random cruelties of Thomas Hardy's novels and Joseph Conrad's Augustan sense of the general vanity of human wishes. Yet the great American novels are somehow consistently bleaker, more often than not ending in disappointment, decline, disillusionment, or even death – in striking contrast to the upbeat notion of the American dream.

What events led to this pessimism? The period 1840 to 1940 was certainly one of bewildering change, with more than 30 million immigrants entering the United States, and central government becoming steadily more powerful and important – a process intensified by the large-scale federal programmes of the New Deal introduced to fight the devastation wrought by the Great Depression.

It's worth noting that, apart from Bigger in *Native Son*, all the victims in the novels we have looked at are well established, long settled, white Americans. Even the poor and marginal, like Huck and Carrie, have some status in the social dispensation. Steinbeck sharpened this focus by having the Joads descended from settler stock derived from Anglo-Saxon origins. Among the migrants in *The Grapes of Wrath* there is no mention of the Mexicans, Filipinos and African Americans who were also part of the documentary history of California farm labour.

What do these sad endings have in common? They all work around the armature of captivity and escape. Most, if not all, the escapes are failures –

that is, either failures to escape (Newland Archer in *The Age of Innocence*) or escapes that go wrong, like Isabel's to Italy, Huck's down the river with Jim, Carrie's, Nick Carraway's to the East, Frederic and Catherine's to Switzerland, Jason Compson's from his family, the Joad family's to California, Bigger Thomas's from his neighbourhood and its racist environment – all these are dashes for different kinds of freedom that end in tears, or worse.

It all may go back to what one might call frontier anxiety – the conflict of exhilaration and anxiety of being on a frontier. Fittingly enough, literary expressions of frontier anxiety figure among the earliest and most popular prose stories to be produced in America, the so-called Indian captivity narratives, like Mary Rowlandson's, published in 1682, which went through four editions that year.

So it was often conceived as part of one's education, a sort of American version of the European grand tour. "We send our youth abroad to grow luxurious and effeminate in Europe," wrote the novelist, diplomat and historian Washington Irving; "it appears to me that a previous tour on the prairies would be more likely to produce that manliness, simplicity and self-dependence, most in unison with our political institutions." Note that the journey was to be a "tour", a rite of passage into American manhood.

So exciting, yet so threatening was the western frontier, that it had to be mythologised in one way or another. Sometimes it was made representative of the whole country, identified with typically American enterprise and freedom.

Which brings us to the one book missing from this list of sad-ending stories, *My Ántonia*. Willa Cather had the wit to deconstruct the myth of the frontier, as both threat and challenge. In *My Ántonia* "manhood" doesn't come into it; it's the women who make the West – and as a place to live, not just visit. The women, too, undergo a kind of initiation, but it's nothing like the rite of passage, as fabled by Washington Irving.

Like the male initiation, it involves suffering and hardship, but it is not based on childish opposition or escape, and if it arouses fear, it's not the fear of the savage Other, but of normal environmental challenges to be overcome by patient settlement and building. And it is figured not on the break from Europe or the American East, but on the cultural continuity of generations, of the Old World and the New. In other words, Cather's West is a site of progressive development, whose cultural links to society and civilisation, though stretched, are not broken. That is why its author could imagine it ending happily.

FURTHER READING

General

Richard Chase, *The American Novel and its Tradition*, Durham, North Carolina: Duke University Press, 1957.

Leslie Fiedler, *Love and Death in the American Novel*, New York: Stein & Day, 1966.

R.W.B. Lewis, *The American Adam: Innocence, Tragedy and Tradition in the Nineteenth Century*, Chicago: University of Chicago Press, 1955.

Leo Marx, *The Machine in the Garden: Technology and the Pastoral Ideal in America*, New York: Oxford University Press, 1964.

Henry Nash Smith, *Virgin Land: The American West as Symbol and Myth*, Cambridge, MA, Harvard University Press, 1950.

Lionel Trilling, "Reality in America," in his *The Liberal Imagination*, New York: Viking Press, 1950.

Ian Watt, *The Rise of the Novel*, London: Chatto and Windus, 1957.

The Portrait of a Lady

Millicent Bell, *Meaning in Henry James*, Cambridge, MA: Harvard University Press, 1991.

Robert D, Bamberg, ed., *Henry James: The Portrait of a Lady*, New York: Norton Critical Editions, 1995.

James Galloway, *Henry James: "The Portrait of a Lady"*, London: Edward Arnold, 1967.

Philip Horne, ed., *Henry James, The Portrait of a Lady*, London: Penguin Books, 2011.

Philip Horne, ed., *Henry James: A Life in Letters*, London: Penguin Books, 1999.

Dorothea Krook, *The Ordeal of Consciousness in Henry James*, Cambridge: Cambridge University Press, 1862.

Tony Tanner, "The Fearful Self: Henry James's *The Portrait of a Lady*," in Tony Tanner, ed., *Henry James: Modern Judgements*, London: Macmillan, 1968.

Huckleberry Finn

Thomas Cooley, ed., *Adventures of Huckleberry Finn*, New York: Norton Critical Editions, 1961.

Ernest Hemingway, *Green Hills of Africa*, New York: Scribner's, 1935.

Kenneth S, Lynn, ed., *Huckleberry Finn: Text, Sources, Criticism*, New York: Harcourt, Brace & World, 1961.

Leo Marx, "Mr. Eliot, Mr. Trilling, and *Huckleberry Finn*," reprinted in *Huckleberry Finn: Text, Sources, Criticism*.

Jane Smiley, "Say It Ain't So, Huck": Second Thoughts on Mark Twain's "Masterpiece," reprinted in the *Norton Critical Edition of Adventures of Huckleberry Finn*.

Sister Carrie

Theodore Dreiser, "Sisters and Suitors," from *Dawn*, New York: Horace Liveright, 1921, reprinted in the Norton Critical edition of *Sister Carrie*.

F. R. Leavis, *Essays and Documents*, ed. Ian MacKillop and Richard Storer, Sheffield, England: Sheffield Academic Press, 1995.

Julian Markels, "Dreiser and the Plotting of Inarticulate Experience," in the Norton Critical Edition of *Sister Carrie*.

F. O. Matthiessen, *Theodore Dreiser*, New York: Sloane, 1951.

Donald Pizer, *Realism and Naturalism in Nineteenth-Century American Literature*, Carbondale, Ill.: Southern Illinois University Press, 1966.

Donald Pizer, ed., *Theodore Dreiser, Sister Carrie,* New York, Norton Critical Editions, 1970.

My Ántonia

Harold Bloom, ed., *Willa Cather's My Ántonia*, New York: Chelsea House, 1987.

David Daiches, *Willa Cather: A Critical Introduction*, Ithaca: Cornell University Press, 1951.

Blanche H. Gelfant, "The Forgotten Reaping Hook: Sex in *My Ántonia*," reprinted in Willa Cather's My Ántonia.

The Age of Innocence

Nancy Bentley, *The Ethnography of Manners: Hawthorne, James, Wharton*, Cambridge: Cambridge University Press, 1995.

Candace Waid, ed., *Edith Wharton, The Age of Innocence*, New York: Norton Critical Editions, 2003.

The Great Gatsby

Letha Audhuy, *The Waste Land* Myth and Symbols in *The Great Gatsby*, in *"The Great Gatsby": Modern Interpretations*.

Marius Bewley, "Scott Fitzgerald's Criticism of America," in *"The Great Gatsby": Modern Interpretations*.

Harold Bloom, ed., *F. Scott Fitzgerald's "The Great Gatsby":Modern Interpretations*. New York: Chelsea House, 1986.

Keath Fraser, "Another Reading of *The Great Gatsby*," in *"The Great Gatsby": Modern Interpretations*.

A. B. Paulson, "Oral Aggression and Splitting," in *"The Great Gatsby": Modern Interpretations*.

David Parker, "Two Versions of the Hero," in *"The Great Gatsby": Modern Interpretations*.

Brian Way, "The Great Gatsby," *F. Scott Fitzgerald and the Art of Social Fiction*, London: Edward Arnold, 1980.

A Farewell to Arms

Scott Donaldson, ed., *New Essays on A Farewell to Arms*, Cambridge: Cambridge University Press, 1990.

Sandra Whipple Spanier, "Hemingway's Unknown Soldier: Catherine Barkley, the Critics and the Great War," in *New Essays on A Farewell to Arms*.

Ben Stoltzfus, "A Sliding Discourse: The Language of *A Farewell to Arms*," in *New Essays on A Farewell to Arms*.

Robert Penn Warren, "Introduction" to Ernest Hemingway, *A Farewell to Arms*, New York: Scribner's, 1949.

The Sound and the Fury

Michael Gorra, ed., William Faulkner, *The Sound and the Fury*, New York: Norton Critical Editions, 2014.

Donald M. Kartiganer, *The Fragile Thread: The Meaning of Form in Faulkner's Novels*, Amherst: University of Massachusetts Press, 1979.

Jean Paul Sartre, "On *The Sound and the Fury*: Time in the Work of Faulkner," in the Norton Critical Edition of *The Sound and the Fury*.

The Grapes of Wrath

Jackson Benson, *The True Adventures of John Steinbeck, Writer*. London: Heinemann, 1984.

Clifton Fadiman, "Highway 66 – A Tale of Five Cities," *The New Yorker*, 15 April, 1939.

Howard Levant, *The Novels of John Steinbeck: A Critical Study*, Columbia, MO: The University of Missouri Press, 1974.

Mary McCarthy, "Minority Report," *The Nation*, March, 1936.

David Wyatt, ed. *New Essays on "The Grapes of Wrath"*, Cambridge: Cambridge University Press, 1990.

Native Son

James Baldwin, "Everybody's Protest Novel" (1949), in James Baldwin, *Notes of a Native Son*, Boston: Beacon Press, 1955.

Burton Rascoe, "Negro Novel and White Reviewers," *The American Mercury*, July, 1940.

John M. Reilly, "Giving Bigger a Voice: The Politics of Narrative in *Native Son*," in Kenneth Kinnamon, *New Essays on "Native Son"*, Cambridge: Cambridge University Press, 1990.

CG CONNELL GUIDES

Concise, intelligent guides to history and literature

CONNELL GUIDES TO LITERATURE

Novels and poetry
Emma
Far From the Madding Crowd
Frankenstein
Great Expectations
Hard Times
Heart of Darkness
Jane Eyre
Lord of the Flies
Mansfield Park
Middlemarch
Mrs Dalloway
Paradise Lost
Persuasion
Pride and Prejudice
Tess of the D'Urbervilles
The Canterbury Tales
The Great Gatsby
The Poetry of Robert Browning
The Waste Land
To Kill A Mockingbird
Wuthering Heights
Shakespeare
A Midsummer Night's Dream
Antony and Cleopatra
Hamlet
Julius Caesar
King Lear

Macbeth
Othello
Romeo and Juliet
The Second Tetralogy
The Tempest
Twelfth Night
Modern texts
A Doll's House
A Room with a View
A Streetcar Named Desire
An Inspector Calls
Animal Farm
Atonement
Beloved
Birdsong
Hullabaloo
Never Let Me Go
Of Mice and Men
Rebecca
Spies
The Bloody Chamber
The Catcher in the Rye
The History Boys
The Road
Vernon God Little
Waiting for Godot
NEW
A Short History of English

Literature
American literature
Dystopian literature
How to write well
How to read Shakespeare
How to read a poem

How to write an essay
The Gothic
The poetry of Christina Rossetti
Women in literature

NEW: CONNELL GUIDES TO HISTORY

Guides
The French Revolution
Winston Churchill
World War One
The Rise and Fall of the Third Reich
The American Civil War
Stalin
Lenin
Nelson
The Tudors
Napoleon

The Cold War
The American Civil Rights Movement
The Normans
Russia and its Rulers

Short Guides
Britain after World War Two
Edward VI
Mary I
The General Strike
The Suffragettes

Connell Guides should be required reading in every school in the country."
Julian Fellowes, creator of Downton Abbey
What Connell Guides do is bring immediacy and clarity: brevity with depth. They unlock the complex and offer students an entry route."
Colin Hall, Head of Holland Park School
These guides are a godsend. I'm so glad I found them."
Jessica Enthoven, A Level student, St Mary's Calne
Completely brilliant. I wish I were young again with these by my side. It's like being in a room with marvellous tutors. You can't really afford to be without them, and they are a joy to read."
Joanna Lumley

To buy any of these guides, or for more information, go to
www.connellguides.com
or contact us on (020)79932644 / info@connellguides.com

First published in 2018 by
Connell Guides
Spye Arch House
Spye Park
Lacock
Wiltshire
SN15 2PR

10 9 8 7 6 5 4 3 2 1

Picture credits:
p.17 © Alamy
p.79 © Alamy

A CIP catalogue record for this book is available from the British Library.
978-1-911187-57-8

Design © Nathan Burton
Assistant Editor and Typeset by:
Paul Woodward

Printed by Short Run Press Ltd, Exeter

www.connellguides.com